# CHINESE FOLK TALES

LOUISE AND YUAN-HSI KUO

# CHINESE FOLK TALES

CELESTIAL ARTS
Millbrae, California

**Interior Art by John Kuo**

First Printing, January 1976
Manufactured in the United States of America

1   2   3   4   5   6   80   79   78   77   76

**Library of Congress Cataloging in Publication Data**

Chinese folktales.

   1. Tales, Chinese—Translations into English.   2. Tales, English—Translations from Chinese.   3. Folk-lore—China.   1. Kuo, Louise.   2. Kuo, Yuan-Hsi.
GR335.C555        398.2'0951        75-9082
ISBN 0-89087-074-8

# Contents

# Foreword

This is the busy, bustling Hong Kong of today. Taxis and double-decker busses carry multitudes of tourists between magnificent hotels and modern high-rise buildings. As in every densely populated major metropolis the world over, city fathers labor over such problems as airport expansion . . . last year saw almost four million passengers through Hong Kong International Airport. Meanwhile, the Advisory Committee on Environmental Pollution works to solve problems resulting from urban growth. Hong Kong is trendy, Western modern dress is visible everywhere; four television channels, predominantly in color, influence the rapid-moving population.

But suddenly the room echoes with an ear-splitting clash of cymbals and the sonorous boom of a drum and in the street below our window prances a splendid lion. The sound of cymbals and the beat of drums have been heard incessantly since early morning and are merely a prelude to the major part to come: a procession with gay silk banners flying, votive offerings of barbecued pigs . . . golden brown and saffron, cartloads heaped with fruit, red-colored eggs and other delicacies, giant *joss sticks* (incense), candles and lanterns. A magnificent dragon, gyrating and performing with vigor and intensity to the rapid beat of a drum, will bring the procession to a climax. Throngs crowd the doorways, line the path, as excited onlookers join the ranks to mingle with those on their way to the temple . . . journey's end. This is the day of days . . . the grand finale to five days of celebration in homage to T'ien Ho, the Heavenly Goddess of the Sea . . . she who will bestow blessings on all who worship her, and protect them for the entire year.

Within the temple, multitudes hold lighted *joss sticks,* kowtow and kneel in supplication before the clay image of T'ien Ho. All who utter a prayer know the folktale of the fisherman's wife who stood on the hilltop of Shatin in Kowloon along the Kwangtung border. Everyone knew that all lives had been lost when the boat capsized during a storm. But she never relinquished hope that her husband would return. Rain or shine, day after day, she climbed to the top of the hill. Often the crash of thunder and flash of lightning broke around her; yet she waited. T'ien Ho took pity on her one day, and with a single stroke of lightning, turned her and the infant on her back into stone. The boulder in a shape resembling mother and child is known as *Wang Fu Shan,* meaning literally, *Awaiting Husband Hill.*

Today many fisherfolk are asking for T'ien Ho's blessing and protection. Others pray for personal favors, good luck, wealth or health. She has become a Goddess of Mercy. The earnest faces, the offerings in the smoke filled room, pungent with incense, and the murmur of prayers, bring to mind the Han folktale, *New Year Offerings,* which you will find included in this book. The festival is a wondrous, age-old event that villagers embellish with fanciful thought, spin tales about and tell over and over as in the past. It is the fabric from which folktales are made.

The folktales in this book are merely a few of the countless stories that were once told throughout China, and later written, edited and compiled by scholars. Some were fanciful while others portrayed the thought and life of the Han people who lived all over China, but especially on the plains and in the fertile Yellow River Valley, regarded as the cradle of the Chinese civilization. Other tales were of the tribespeople, who did not have a very good relation with the Han rulers in the past, and were driven to the hinterland where they survived, and managed to retain their age-old customs and traditions against manifold odds. Many stories revolved around their superstitions and early beliefs; some described the troublous beginnings of the world, the calamities that beset mankind or accounted for strange phenomena. Others revealed wishful thinking, for better life, more money and so forth. Many folktales contained animals, birds and insects that were used as simile with a lesson such as Aesop's Fables.

This compilation was translated from Chinese texts. Various writers, some known, others anonymous, edited the tales and translated them from an archaic prose form into modern language. They are what their name implies, simply tales of common folk rather than stories with classic, literary background although some were the inspiration for such tales. It is hoped they will arouse the interest of the reader to learn more about China's inhabitants from Central Asia; the nomads called Scythians by the Greeks, a warlike, adventurous, artistic people who wandered far into Eastern Asia and from whom the Chinese received their first known contact with European people; and more about the national minorities for without them,

China's more than five thousand years of history would be incomplete.

China is comprised of multiracial groups that include the Han and national minorities. Of the eight hundred million population of the People's Republic of China the Han constitute ninety-four percent and live chiefly in Central China, known as China Proper. The remaining six percent represent over fifty national minorities of varied ethnic origins. The forebears of some were related to the Turks and Tatars, and lived in the (present) Mongolian steppe; others were of Tungus stock from the Amur basin region; yet others were from Southwest Asia—Babylonia, according to some scholars.

The first emperor, known to posterity as Huang Ti, The Yellow Emperor, ruled over the fertile Yellow River Valley. Before acquiring his exalted status he was a powerful chieftain, allegedly a descendent of the Hua Hsia tribe. The fierce battle to decide the tribal supremacy and control over these vital regions, was fought between Huang Ti's tribe and another tribal leader, Ch'ih Yu, whose forebears came from regions outside China. The victor was Huang Ti and his descendants were known as the Han.

## THE HAN PEOPLE AND THEIR FOLKTALES

The Han people, who dominated China Proper, attained a high degree of culture and contributed to the civilization of mankind in such fields as philosophy, science, literature, ceramics, painting, sculpture, medicine and astrology. Among their inventions are listed the printing press, block prints, the lunar calendar, paper, gunpowder, firecrackers, and acupuncture used for anaesthesia.

Both the Han common people and the ruling class listened with never failing interest to storytellers reciting folktales. Whereas court scribes left official records to glorify the sovereign and dynasty, the folktales often revealed another side of the story. Scholars who were critical of the orthodox way of writing history, found a fresh approach in the unadorned tales and recorded them. With the advancement of culture, they were enhanced and converted into writing of literary merit.

The true feelings of the common man, his inner thought and aspirations were conveyed by such tales. Joy, sorrow, hardship, greed, fear and varied emotions were portrayed simply yet skillfully; often with roguish humor. Religious beliefs, superstitions, morals, ethics and philosophy were popular topics that showed the social conditions, manners, customs and thought of people during a particular era. With the rise and fall of the dynasties, living conditions differed as did viewpoints toward life. These, among other things can be detected in the tales. One can even read ancient history in a different light and understand why at certain periods there was enlightenment whereas at others, a revolt was brewing. Time and again, discontent with the prevailing government or hatred of an alien king, were voiced in the stories, although the real thoughts were disguised by allegories and metaphors. The common people understood what was implied; officials usually did too, but were powerless to punish anyone. In any case, such folktales, coupled with superstitious prophesies, were used as an instrument to stir up a massive revolt or to fan discontent, and instances showed that they hastened the downfall of the dynasty.

## THE CHINESE NATIONAL MINORITIES
## AND THEIR FOLKTALES

After the battle with Huang Ti, the defeated southern tribes, called the *Nan Man* (southern barbarians) by the victorious Han, retreated to the mountainous regions of Kwangtung in the south, and Kwangsi, Yunnan, Szechuan, Kweichow and Tibet in the southwest. Other nomadic tribes dwelt in Sinkiang, Ch'inghai (Tsinghai), Kansu, Ninghsia and Inner Mongolia of the northwestern regions. In addition some lived in the northeastern provinces of Manchuria. (See Map pages 174-175.) There are over fifty tribes, presently known as the Chinese National Minorities, living on the perimeter of China Proper (the central part of China).

The minorities had vastly different cultures from the Han. Their heritage, history and environment were greatly responsible for the distinctions. They were not bound by traditional rules to regulate thought and behavior as with the Han, and freely expressed themselves in song and dance. Their music was a very interesting part of their cultures. Some of the musical instruments originated in the dim past but are still used for their songs and dances that generally portray the life and thought of the tribespeople. The splendid designs and fascinating colors of their costumes, and handicrafts such as basketry, pottery, weaving and paper cuts, to mention only a few, reveal exceptional talent. They have incredible artistic skill in embroidery, and apply this to daily articles as well as their dress. Some of the minorities excel in one field above the others, but all have a high degree of natural aptitude in the crafts that include the making of jewelry and carpets.

The hard life of the minorities was reflected in their folktales, that contained an element of wishful thinking and magic, bringing sudden good fortune, bounty and happiness . . . similar to the "Arabian Nights' Tales." The wish for a better life, a strong or handsome spouse, a capable, kind daughter-in-law, freedom or justice were ordinary yearnings but were converted into tales having a high level of poetic feeling and imagination.

A less hardy people would not have survived. Yet retreating to the hinterland helped the minorities retain their social customs and native ways of life and thus their cultures did survive. But so too did their hatred for the Han. The folktales used metaphors to express this in a very subtle way.

The minorities had valid reasons to fear and hate the wealthy, powerful Han, a major one being an official's liberty to take possession of whatever attracted him. The minority folktales often recounted those misfortunes. Some of the most ancient tales attributed a woman's pregnancy to her meeting a dragon, being waylaid by the creature, or to eating a bright red mulberry, as illustrated in one of our early tales, *The Golden Sheng.* How much was symbolic containing an element of truth or merely superstition is debatable. Superstition most certainly affected the peoples' lives and their isolation and privations colored the tales. It should also be remembered that the dragon was a symbol of Han imperial authority and always portrayed as a benevolent creature by the Han, whereas the minorities usually depicted it as evil because it stood as a symbol of the imperial might of the Han.

## CHINA TODAY

The fears, hatred and isolation of the minorities are happily things of the past. The people are no longer exploited by the Han or looked down on as second rate citizens, but treated as equals. Former illiterate peasants are being taught to read and write, and use modern technical methods and equipment. Opportunities for education from the primary school to the university are open to them exactly as the Han people with whom they live in harmony and peace. The former humiliating designation "barbarians," has been replaced by "Chinese National Minorities," and they call each other "brother." In the varied regions where the national minorities dwell, national self-government has been established. Working side by side with the Han in all fields of endeavor, they have become a part of the mainstream of Chinese culture. Moreover, a genuine effort has been made for them to retain the worthy aspects of their own cultures. To this end, the People's Republic of China founded an academy with headquarters in Peking, devoted to the study of the minority cultures, and their talents are encouraged to create living art forms. Recently similar academies have been established in other cities.

The questions that remain unanswered and solutions sought for many issues that revolve around minorities are pertinent to conditions in other parts of the world. The Chinese have solved their age-old problem with perception and understanding. It is worthy of study to learn their way. Hatred, grievances, resentments, and discontent have their roots in the past as the folktales so poignantly reveal.

Perhaps nowhere so much as within present-day mainland China are new types of folktales being created; they reflect the vast changes in the lives of the Han and of the national minorities. Today's stories are generally shorter for here as in other countries, people lead busy lives. But since Han and minority music, songs and dances have been incorporated into the repertoire; it has given the Han people a chance to learn about the minority cultures, and the minorities to understand the Han. The themes vary; some relate to heroic struggles of the peoples' revolution; others depict the harvest celebration; some tell about the achievements of present leaders and so forth. The life of today is the folktale of tomorrow, but a part of yesteryear is inevitably interwoven into them.

The authors hope these folktales will arouse the interest of the reader to learn more about the historical background and culture of China—the ancient Middle Kingdom, as well as the present People's Republic of China.

—Louise & Yuan-hsi Kuo

# The First Storyteller

*A Han Folktale*

Story telling goes back to time immemorial. In ancient times, a minstrel traveled about the country much as was depicted in this tale. A musical instrument such as a *p'i-p'a*, clappers, a drum, or fiddle, accompanied his tale; at times just a large folding fan, to stress the rhythm, that was opened with a forceful flourish at decisive points and closed with a resounding snap. The style of relating a story was almost as important as the tale itself.

Legends about the world's beginnings and creation of mankind, sage kings, and evil ones; folk tales about historical personages; culture heroes, poets, and philosophers; and episodes from historical romances were immensely popular. There were also instances of exiled kings who lived happily among the common people; of scholars, disillusioned with court life and officialdom who found happiness and spiritual comfort living in reclusion despite physical deprivations.

All were generally included in the extensive repertoire of an itinerant, professional storyteller whose narrations provided entertainment and popular education throughout the length and breadth of the land. Wending his way through dusty lanes to the click clack of clappers, he possessed the magnetic attraction of the Pied Piper of Hamlin.

This tale is about the very first storyteller. It was said that he was a king's son, blind at birth. As soon as the king was told, he ordered the infant to be abandoned for he wanted a more worthy successor to his throne.

The baby was taken to a high mountain where many wild animals roamed, and left there to die. Strange to say, they did not harm him, but took pity on him and

13

brought him to their caves. The tiger and leopard suckled him, the fox helped to clothe him, the mountain goat provided sandals, and the pheasant, a covering for his head. The mountain and earth gods told him stories, and the sweet singing oriole taught him how to sing. He grew to be strong and wise, able to relate wondrous stories and sing melodies most pleasing to hear.

After seven years had elapsed, a jade *p'i-p'a* dropped from heaven into his lap. A fairy living in the forest, taught him how to play, and soon he became an expert minstrel; none could excel him. So one day, he carefully wrapped his *p'i-p'a* and bid farewell to his friends.

In his wanderings, he met shepherds, hunters, peasants and farmers. He played his *p'i-p'a* for them, sang and related stories such as they had never before heard. In turn, they gave him sustenance and shelter, and unfolded stories about their lives. This enabled him to understand the sorrows and joys of life and thus create many more stories that brought laughter and tears to all his listeners.

After a time, he met a scholar who spoke about astrology, geology, the ancient classics and teachings of the sages. Thereafter his story telling was even more eloquent and stirring. Wherever he went, people became his friend and treated him like a brother. Days and years went by in just this way.

One day, because of him, now a splendid youth of sixteen, a serious quarrel arose between two very wealthy herdsmen, originally good friends. One, a cattle owner, had listened to the youth sing and tell stories, and afterward could not bear to part with him. For scores of days, the young boy was retained to sing and relate an inexhaustible fund of stories.

The other, a horse owner, visited one day, and at once was so taken with the youth's ability that he became obsessed with the wish to have the minstrel live with him.

But the cattle owner persistently refused to allow the storyteller to go away. Thereupon the two friends started to argue and then came to blows. However, the horse owner succeeded in fleeing with the youth. The cattle owner became so upset that he petitioned the king to judge the case and punish the horse owner. In turn, his former friend quickly lodged a complaint saying that he was injured in the unjust fight.

The king listened to their arguments that carried on for three days and nights. Since both men had good reasons for their behavior, the minstrel was ordered to the palace for questioning.

"What are you carrying?" the king inquired.

"My *p'i-p'a*."

The curious king requested the boy to play. When he plucked the strings and sang, the king sat entranced. Then the youth was asked to tell his stories. One followed the other; one song came after the other, each surpassing the previous one. For three days and nights, the officials, princesses and court attendants surrounded him, entreating him to continue.

"There will be no end to this," the king thought. "Moreover, it is deviating from my original intention to listen to the case. I'll ask him to tell us something about himself, and perhaps learn how he happened to be the subject of this dispute."

The blind youth did not know who the king was, and freely described how he had been abandoned by heartless parents but was saved by the kindly animals and birds of the forest. "The mountain and earth gods told me the story," he said, "and many others too."

Everyone in the palace realized that he was the abandoned crown prince, and wept until he finished his story.

"He is our only son!" the king and queen cried.

"In spite of his blindness," the king announced, "he

will be the wisest of sovereigns and the true successor to my throne."

But the storyteller was unwilling to live in the palace. No one could persuade him to stay and he took leave to roam from place to place telling stories to his friends and brothers.

And tales of the storyteller soon were heard. It was said that by and by he met a beggar limping along with great difficulty. Taking two splints from his own leg supports, he gave them to the beggar. He also taught him how to sing running verse. The beggar eventually shortened the splints and by placing them between his fingers, kept time while singing and reciting verse. The clap of the castenets was so spirited and pleasant to hear that people called his type of singing, "falling petals of a lotus flower," and eventually it became a special type of story telling.

It was also said that by taking one of the strings from his *p'i-p'a* he helped devise a measuring rod for Lu Pan who later was worshipped as the Father of Carpentry, and of whom many tales were told concerning his unusual ability to build bridges, houses, moving battlements for war and all types of construction requiring engineering feats.

Another string from the *p'i-p'a* he gave to the old and renowned scholar and philosopher Chiang T'ai Kung so that he could fish in the River Wei. That is why the *p'i-p'a'* has only four strings now instead of the original six. And, it is the reason that ever since then the storyteller, the fisherman and the carpenter have a very special friendly relationship with each other.

# The Golden Sheng

*A Miao Folktale*

Two and a half million Miao people are scattered throughout Hunan, Kwangtung, Kwangsi, Yunnan, Kweichow and Szechuan Provinces. A southern minority, the differences in apparel, headdress and ornaments are fascinating. Although all minorities dress in a distinctive style, the Miao costumes are outstanding. The embroidery on them reveals the women's artistry and incredible skill. Her skirt and blouse, a man's sash (often presented to the man of her choice as a pledge of love) and all sorts of articles for daily use are embroidered.

The Sheng, the musical instrument that the Miao sang and danced to, was a most ancient one. The Chou Dynasty Book of Rites mentioned it as being used during the ceremonies for the worship of heaven, earth, and the ancestors; for rites performed for the four seasons, and supplications for rain and a good harvest. It was used as a solo instrument but low or medium pitched pipes have now been designed for orchestral work. Generally made of bamboo, the pipes vary from a foot to two feet; the sound is produced by blowing and sucking air through a brass cup-like base that clasps the pipes.

The dragon was the oldest known symbol in China, and was worshipped as the rain spirit that controlled the springtime. It was a symbol of fertility and rebirth, and was regarded as a beneficient creature. But when the sovereign of the yellow earth district ruled, he chose the dragon as his imperial emblem. The defeated chieftain of the southern tribes had the phoenix as his emblem; others had the tortoise and unicorn. These creatures were reclassified during the Han Dynasty according to their importance, and the dragon was elevated to a supreme position that signified not only the imperial power of the sovereign, but stood for the Han people themselves, a racial distinction. Therefore, as in this folktale the southern tribes generally depicted the dragon as evil and cruel. To them, it stood as a symbol of the victorious Han and the hated official with whom there were many conflicts.

There was once a mother and daughter who lived in a hut on a hillside. The little girl liked to dress in red (which is the color symbolizing happiness) so she was called Little Red Maiden. One day when they were working in the fields, a gust of wind suddenly came from nowhere. A frightening dragon appeared in the sky, snatched the maiden and flew toward the east. The mother heard her daughter's voice drifting with the wind, faintly calling, "Save Little Red Maiden—depending on little brother. Ma-ma, remember . . . "

The helpless mother could only shed tears. "I have only a daughter. Where is any younger brother?" she sobbed as she stared at the vacant sky. Dragging herself along in a daze, she stumbled homeward. Halfway home, her hair caught on a mulberry branch. While disentangling the strands, she noticed a bright red mulberry and automatically picked it and popped it into her mouth.

After a few days, she gave birth to a round-headed little boy with rosy cheeks, and named him Mulberry Boy. He grew so fast that within a short time, he was as big as a lad of fifteen. The mother often thought of sending him to save his sister; yet she was reluctant to have him encounter any danger. So she just wept each day in secret. But one day a black crow flew to the eave of their hut and sang:

> *Your sister is suffering; your sister is suffering,*
> *In the evil dragon's cave.*
> *Tears cover her face;*
> *Blood stains her back;*
> *Her hand drills the rock.*
> *Your sister is suffering; your sister is suffering.*

Mulberry Boy heard the song and asked, "Ma-ma, do I have a sister?"

"Yes, my child. Your sister was fond of wearing a red dress, and was called Little Red Maiden. She was seized by a wicked dragon who has already killed so many people," she replied tearfully.

"I'll kill the evil dragon. I must save my sister—save all the people," he cried out as he picked up a big wooden stick to go in search of the dragon.

He journeyed until he reached a path on the hillside where he saw a large, pointed boulder. There was no way to pass except to climb over it, but if not careful he would slip and injure himself. "This is a tiger by the wayside. It will harm many people if I don't destroy it," Mulberry Boy thought as he took his stick to give it a whack. There was a crack, but nothing broke except the stick.

Thereupon, he crouched low, used both hands to push with all his might and sent the boulder rolling down into the valley. Ah! A dazzling golden sheng was revealed exactly where the boulder had been. He picked it up and began to blow on it. What a brilliant, melodious sound! Suddenly, the earthworms, frogs and lizards all along the roadside began to dance. The faster he played, the faster they danced. As soon as the music ceased, they also stopped. "Umm, now I have a way of dealing with that noxious dragon," Mulberry Boy thought to himself, and kept on walking until he reached the edge of a big, rocky mountain where the ferocious, evil dragon could be seen curled up in front of a stone cave. Nearby were piles of bones and skulls, and a girl in a dress of red. Her cheeks were stained with tears, and in her hand was an iron pick that she used to chisel the cave. The dragon used his tail to flip against her back while he sang:

*Wa, wa, foolish maiden,*
*To marry (me) you say nay;*
*Drill, drill, drill away*
*Drill the rocks everyday.*
*Unable to chisel through the mountain,*
*Your life, I will not spare.*

"This maiden must be my sister," Mulberry thought and called aloud,

*Evil dragon, evil dragon, torturing my sister!*
*Day after day, I will play*
*On my golden sheng.*
*Never will I stop, and your life I will not spare!*

Mulberry Boy then began to play and the wicked dragon involuntarily began to dance. Little Red Maiden threw away the pick and ran to watch. She wanted to converse with her brother, but he raised his hand to quiet her. As he played faster and faster, the dragon stretched his back and whirled ever faster. Fire came from his eyes; puffs of smoke rolled from his nostrils, and sounds of exhaustion issued from his mouth. "Oh, oh, little brother, stop playing," he pleaded. "Don't torture me. I'll let your sister go. Spare my life."

Now how in the world would Mulberry Boy ever consent to stop? He kept on playing as he walked toward a large, steep cliff. The dragon followed, dancing and swirling round and round. There was a thunderous crash and the dragon fell into the pond below. But this did not stop him from dancing. On and on he danced until he was so weary, fire streamed from his eyes; smoke billowed from his nostrils and dreadful sounds of exhaustion came from his mouth. "Ow, ow, little brother, spare me this once," he begged piteously. "I'll stay in the depths of the pond and never commit any wrong."

"Evil dragon, you evil one! Listen to what I have to say—stay at the bottom of the deep pond and don't ever again dare to create trouble."

The dragon nodded and promised. Mulberry Boy stopped playing, and the dragon slithered to the bottom of the pond. Mulberry Boy then took his sister's hand; both smiled happily, and walked away. But they had not gone far when they heard a sound like a thunderclap, and turning around, saw the dragon emerging with claws outstretched to pounce on them.

Little Red Maiden counselled her brother, "When digging a well, dig deep; when weeding grass, dig out the root. As long as the evil dragon is alive, he will harm people."

Mulberry Boy quickly went to the edge of the water to play the golden sheng. With that, the evil dragon involuntarily went into the pond, danced, twisted and whirled to the tune of the music. Mulberry Boy played with ever increasing speed for seven days and nights without stopping. The dragon finally collapsed and died and floated on the surface of the pond.

The sister and brother laughed happily as they dragged the dragon's body home. When their mother saw them returning, she laughed until her mouth could hardly close. They used the dragon's skin to repair the roof; his bones as a post and beam to support the roof, and his horns for a plow. The fields were plowed so rapidly, an ox was no longer necessary. They plowed many fields and planted great quantities of greens and thereafter lived a comfortable happy life.

# How the Horse-Head Fiddle Was Created

*A Mongolian Folktale*

There are approximately one and a half million Mongolian people. Some of them live in Ch'inghai and Kansu Provinces, but the majority reside in the Inner Mongolian autonomous area. In the past, their sovereign, a Kahn, ruled over the people, who were mainly herdsmen or breeders of horses, cattle and sheep. Wherever the animals roamed, the men would follow, living as nomads in *yurts*. When caravan troops met each other, they would exchange tales. But long, solitary journeys from oasis to oasis was a lonely life, and to compensate, they would sing and play music. Their favorite instrument, a fiddle with a horse-head adorning the top and snakeskin over the sounding board, is known as a *Tartar violin* in China.

How was the Mongolian fiddle, our most popular musical instrument created? Why was it decorated with the head of a horse? This is a very sad story.

There was once an orphan boy named Suho who lived in the Chahar district. His grandmother brought him up, and he helped her with the meals and other household chores besides taking the sheep to graze. They had a score of sheep, but that was all. When Suho came of age at seventeen, he was a lovable lad with a talent for singing. The neighboring herdsmen often gathered in the evening to hear his songs of the pastureland.

One night, Suho failed to return. His grandmother and all the neighbors became quite worried as it grew late. The night was pitch black when Suho finally appeared with a small thing cradled in his arms. It was a pure white newborn foal!

Seeing all the bewildered, anxious faces around him, Suho said, "I saw this little white thing alone and help-less on the roadside. There was no sign of the mare. I was so afraid the wolves would get him that I brought him with me."

Suho gave loving care to the colt, and as time went by, it grew strong and beautiful. Everyone who set eyes on it, loved it. But, of course, it was especially dear to Suho.

One night, Suho was awakened by persistent neighing. Getting up from his sleep, he rushed from the *yurt*. He could hear great confusion and bleating in the sheepfold. The white pony was defending the sheep from a large, gray wolf. Suho drove the wolf away, and turned to the pony. It must have been fighting for a long time. He could see it was exhausted and dripping with sweat.

"Oh, you white pony! Such a good fellow! You have saved the sheep," he said as he tenderly patted the horse and wiped down the sweat. He spoke gently as though addressing his dearest human friend. From that time on the two were never separated, not even for a moment.

One spring, the Khan announced that there would be a horse race and the winner would marry his daughter. The news spread over the pastureland, and Suho's friends urged him to join the race.

On the day of the event, many strong, good-looking young men, dressed in their best, came riding on their steeds of varied colors. Suho had decided to compete and arrived with his snow-white pony. At a given signal, the horses were off, galloping with the speed of a whirlwind. But the white pony was the first to reach the winning post.

"Call the rider of the white pony here," the Khan ordered from the viewing stand. When he saw that the winner was only a simple herdsman, there was no men-

tion of the marriage, and instead he said, "You will be given three big ingots of silver for your horse. You may go home."

"What! Does he really think I'd part with my dearest companion?" Suho thought to himself in anger. But he answered curtly, "I have won the hand of your daughter. I have not come to sell my pony."

"You rascal! How dare a poor herdsman talk to me like this! Seize him!"

Suho was beaten unconscious and lay there until the crowds dispersed and friends came to take him away. The beautiful white pony was led away in triumph by the Khan.

Suho was nursed back to health by his grandmother, and within a short time, recovered completely.

Some days later when Suho was resting, he heard knocking and called out, "Who's there?" Nobody answered but the knocking persisted whereupon his grandmother went outside to see.

"Oh, it's your white pony!" she called out in surprise.

Suho dashed from the *yurt*. He was so happy to see his pony. But happiness turned to grief when he saw seven or eight arrows piercing the body of his dear pony. Gritting his teeth, Suho stiffled his own cry of pain as he pulled out the arrows. Blood instantly streamed from the wounded pony who died the next day.

What had happened? Well, the Khan was overjoyed that he had acquired the splendid white pony, and gave a banquet to celebrate, and exhibit the fine animal to his family and the nobles. When he tried to mount, the pony reared and threw him to the ground. Then it galloped at full speed through the circle of guests.

"Catch it! If you can't catch it, kill it!"the infuriated Khan ordered.

A shower of arrows rained on the helpless pony. But it managed to return to die near its own master.

How sad and unhappy Suho was! He mourned the loss of his pony, day and night, and could not sleep or rest.

One night as he lay tossing, he seemed to see the white pony as though alive. It came right up to him and he fussed over it, caressing it tenderly.

"Can't you think of a way for me to be with you always, dear master?" the pony asked, and after a while said, "Make a fiddle with my bones."

The following morning Suho carved a likeness of his beloved pony's head from its bones, and used it for the upper part of the fiddle. He used its tendons for strings, and the hairs from its flowing tail for the bowstrings.

Whenever Suho played on the horse-head fiddle, the memory of his dearest friend came back to him. His hatred for the Khan increased as he recalled the unfair treatment. These thoughts went into his music and echoed all the desires and emotions of the herdsmen. Every night after work, people flocked to hear him play. Listening, they would forget their weariness of the day.

# The Magic Pole

*A Yi Folktale*

Over three million Yi people reside in Yünnan, Szechwan and Kweichow Provinces. A most artistic people, their headdress has many interesting variations and their attire is adorned with lovely embroidery having age-old patterns often found in Grecian motifs. Similar to other minorities, they love to sing and dance. During the harvest celebrations they hold singing contests and perform their national dances. A simple musical instrument made of grass or a leaf, known as the mouth harp, is very popular with the Yi people. The T'ang Dynasty poet, Pai Chu-yi, described this type of folk music in one of his poems:

*She twists a silver ring out of a willow branch,*
*And with a curling leaf makes music like a jade flute.*

The Chuang, Miao, Pai and others use this ancient, primitive way of making music although some of the Miao use a large fish scale which is actually better as it does not become soft so easily and produces a more resonant sound.

K'unming, in Yünnan Province where this folktale originated, is noted for its beautiful lake, Tien Chih (K'unming Lake). Equally famous is the fair weather all year round. The clear atmosphere and blue sky with unusual cloud formations and their ever-changing shapes have inspired many folktales.

The water in the beautiful K'unming Lake is so clear and blue that the distant mountains and floating clouds always form a perfect double image in the lake. The nearby village cowherds used to bring their cows to graze by the side of the lake while they themselves would lie down to relax, watching the white clouds and dreaming about fairies riding behind the fleecy forms.

One herd of ninety-nine cows brought there to graze

every morning, numbered a hundred by noon and a lovely maiden would appear. But when the cowherds were ready to leave at sunset there would be only ninety-nine and the maiden also, would have disappeared. No one ever understood how this happened. However, the cowherds were very fond of the mysterious maiden who told them many strange tales and seemed to have a knowledge of many things.

One day the maiden said, "There is a magic cow among your herd. It can walk on the surface of water or make it part and a road appear. Whoever rides on its back need never fear crossing any lake. A single hair from its body can carry ten thousand catties." (Approximately 13,333 pounds.)

Of course, all the cowherds were eager to know which was the magic cow. But she would not tell them and said, "Only the honest can benefit by it."

One day when the herd had grazed far beyond their usual ground and trespassed in the field of a poor farmer, he took the old cracked pole used for carrying wood and herded the cows one by one, from the field. By dusk the old farmer was ready to go home. Gathering two bundles of twigs for each end of his pole, he lifted the burden to get along. "Whatever makes it so light today!" he exclaimed. So he added many, many more. But the load was still very light. Finally he piled the wood so high it rose far above his head. Even then he could lift it so easily, it seemed almost weightless, and he made his way home cheerfully at a fast trot.

From then on the old farmer cut wood and every day took it in great stacks to sell in the city. He earned so much money that for the first time in his life, he was able to put some aside.

A rich merchant happened to notice the old man carrying the load and wondered, 'How can an old man carry such a heavy burden and even run along so easily?' So he approached the fellow and asked him.

"This is a magic pole," the old man answered.

Of course the merchant did not believe him but thought, "If what he says is true I'd like to try it." The old man was willing to let him see for himself and much to his amazement found it was really very light. "Ah, I must have the pole," he thought and began to think of a tricky way to wrangle it from the old farmer. But the old man refused to part with it. At last the merchant said, "I'll give you five hundred pieces of silver if you let me have your magic pole."

"Five hundred pieces of silver!" the old farmer exclaimed. "That would be enough for the rest of my life!" With that he handed over the pole.

The merchant glowed with joy over the bargain, but after examining the pole he noted it was cracked and rough. This worried him but he decided, "A good carpenter can plane it smooth." He quickly found a fellow for the job and stood watching until he felt quite satis-, fied. It was now smooth and straight. All the magic hairs that had been caught in the cracks had been planed away too! The pole was now useless! But how could he know that?

His wife was surprised to find him so cheerful that evening and asked, "What has happened? You appear so elated today."

"I bought a magic pole. Try it." Not wishing her to exert herself, he placed a mere ten catties (about thirteen pounds) at each end. Lifting the pole she reproached him, "Magic pole indeed! What kind of foolishness are you talking?"

But the merchant was not concerned for he thought, "Foolishness indeed! What kind of nonsense is she talking?" He added several tens of catties to try himself—to no avail. He could not budge it. The magic had gone from the pole forever.

# The Official and The Hermit

*A Han Folktale*

During the Chou Dynasty when Lao-tze was the "Keeper of the Archives" there were signs that the sovereign was losing control of the vassals, and the dynasty appeared to be crumbling. In despair of being able to help, Lao-tze left his official post, renounced all worldly matters and went to live as a recluse. The Tao Te Ching that he allegedly wrote, formed the basis for the philosophy known as Taoism. Whoever sought the "Way and Virtuous Path of Tao" followed the teachings of Lao-Tze. In every dynasty thereafter, a conscientious official, a frustrated scholar or any disappointed individual, often copied this pattern. It became a way of life to withdraw from the hollow, corrupt, degenerate life of the court or officialdom. This was frowned upon by men who followed the teachings of Confucius.

Whereas Confucius spoke of rules and regulations to establish social order and harmony in life, Lao-tze emphasized living in harmony with the natural order of the universe and said, "Regulations and laws merely reflect the frailties of human behavior. Let each person perfect his own life, and order will prevail." Confucius believed in involvement and action rather than withdrawal and inaction. Their beliefs and way of thinking were poles apart. Yet it has been said that there is a little of the Taoist in every Chinese, and though politicians, bankers or merchants may publicly denounce this way of life, they secretly admire it and read Taoist philosophy in private.

The ancient superstitious belief in predestination and unseen forces intermingle with the philosophy of Confucius and Tao, in this tale. The down to earth reasoning, so characteristic of the Chinese, was revealed in the amusing incident of the boy's appearance on the riverbank. No unseen forces guided the boat but the former servant boy was sent to bring the two friends together. As bosom friends, each was courteous, modestly disclaiming any attainment in life. The Confucian scholar admired the hermit and vice versa, but each went his own way in the end.

Fung Ch'ung and T'ang Yi were schoolmates and very close friends from the same city in Honan Province. Both came from distinguished families and were learned scholars. But their aspirations were quite different. Fung typified the scholar imbued with the classic teachings. He always abided by the social rules and traditions, was courteous, meek and never criticized people or gossiped. T'ang was genial, chivalrous, a knight errant with the spirit of a galloping horse. He was muscular and strong, capable of bending a bow that required the strength of two hundred *catties*. His arrow could hit a target without fail, within a hundred paces. Their diverse interests and personalities seemed to complement each other and sealed a firm bond of friendship.

One day they set out together to enjoy the beauty of the countryside. They chose a quiet, secluded spot near a cascade where they could rest and chat. Fung picked up a pebble and casually aiming at a willow branch, said, "Let's see if it hits the branch to forecast my fortune and future success." The pebble actually hit the mark. This was surely fortuitous!

"Congratulations! Congratulations!" his friend exclaimed. At that moment a small bird darted over the treetop and T'ang murmured, "I'll also cast my fortune."

No sooner was this said, when he shot an arrow swiftly toward the sky. Alas! The bird flew away, and the arrow fell into the creek. T'ang broke his bow, threw the arrows on the ground, and shouted, "Finished!"

"We are only joking," Fung said trying to console him. "Why do you take it so seriously?"

"I can hit a target one hundred times without fail. But today has to be the one day I miss! It is predestined. I've made up my mind."

That year Fung joined the first public examination, and passed. The next year he again passed, this time with honor, and was awarded the title of *Tsin-tze* (similar to the degree of doctor). T'ang, however, wandered among the mountains and rivers without any intention of taking part in the public examination for martial art, and turned a deaf ear on Fung's friendly advice and persuasion.

When Fung was later appointed to an official post in Fukien Province, he sent a messenger asking T'ang to accompany him. But T'ang ignored this kindness and never even gave the courtesy of a reply. Then he left home for an undisclosed destination.

The memory of his good friend always made Fung sad and brought forth a sigh. Whenever there was a festival, he dispatched servants with gifts to look after T'ang's family. He kept this up for over ten years. Yet there was no news of T'ang.

One day Fung bought a houseboy who turned out to be very obstinate and lazy, doing nothing but eat and sleep. Somebody advised Fung to get rid of the boy, but Fung replied, "The boy is still young. Just because his master was changed, doesn't necessarily mean that he would change his habits and obey orders."

One night a band of robbers descended from the rooftop and entered Fung's house. Their faces were covered with masks, and each one carried a knife. The whole household was awakened, but no one knew what to do. Only the boy seemed to know. Jumping from his bed, he raised his arms and let out a fearful growl like an enraged tiger. He grabbed hold of their wrists and broke them, one by one, and then hurled all the robbers over the garden wall. Everyone stood dumfounded by the boy's feat. He had saved the entire family. After the confusion subsided, Fung gave an order to fetch the boy. But he was nowhere to be found.

Some years later Fung resigned his position and sent his family back to his native town while he hired a small boat to visit his relatives and friends up the Yangtze River. The boat was tied to the wharf at the riverport, Ching-ko, for the night. At midnight the anchorage broke loose and the boat began to drift with the current as if guided by an unseen force. In the dark of night there was no way of knowing what direction the boat was taking. But it must have traveled hundreds of *li*, and the boatmen feared everyone would be drowned. When dawn came the boat suddenly ceased moving—stopped at a sandbar. On the bank of the river, there stood the boy who had disappeared from his household. Fung was astonished when without any ceremony, the boy called out, "My master has been waiting for you a long time."

"Who is your master?" Fung asked with curiosity.

"You will know when you see him," he answered, and led the way. After going many *li* through a forest, treading over pine needles, passing murmuring streams and several mountaintops, they reached an opening, "My old friend," a voice called from the cliff, "I haven't seen you for many years." The crystal clear sound penetrated the veil of thin air.

Looking up, Fung saw a saintly figure on the top of the cliff. He wore a robe of plain cloth and a headdress which flowed gently in the breeze imparting an ethereal grace. He was none other than the long departed friend, T'ang Yi. The mere sight of him brought tears of emotion. The cliff looked ever so steep and unattainable. But suddenly a hempen ladder was lowered and the boy helped Fung to mount. After reaching the summit, the two friends embraced and wept.

Fung observed that there were only a few thatched huts and two attendants, the boy being one of them. A stone bench, pinewood table, stove and an ancient guitar were the sole earthly possessions inside the hut. Fung asked

T'ang what had happened after their separation. To this query T'ang answered simply, "I traveled along until I reached this mountain. Fond of its beauty, serenity and spaciousness, I decided to stay. I was afraid that I might never see you again so I sent my boy to attend your house." Only then did Fung realize that his friend possessed deep insight into the unknown, and had already perceived years ago that something would happen in his household, and he sighed.

"You wander proudly and sing amidst the cloud and mist. You retreat, living among the mountains and forest," he said after a reflective pause. "As for me, I am still laboring in the ocean of dust. Compared to you, I am far, far behind."

"On the contrary, my friend," T'ang replied. "You are destined to have wealth and authority, to benefit mankind, to relieve sorrow and bestow good fortune on people. What use am I? My unconventional step achieved nothing. Rambling, roaming, lost amidst hills and rivers—this is just an escape from the world, a means to preserve myself. It is the result of despair, a contradiction of reality. What is there to admire?"

T'ang afterward led Fung down the cliff through fragrant pines, over zigzag footpaths and murmuring creeks until they reached the bank of the river. There they sadly parted.

# New Year Offerings

*A Han Folktale*

The herbalist, Taoist priest and merchant in this folktale, supposedly worked in one way or another for the benefit of the village folk. But they were exposed as hypocrites, equally selfish and greedy with no compassion for their fellowmen. Money was the "Bitch Goddess" and all worshipped at her shrine. The place chosen to betray their true nature was ironically in the Kuan Ti Temple.

Kuan Yu, the general famed for serving Liu Pei, the contender for the throne during the Three Kingdoms Period, was later deified and known as Kuan Ti. He was deified a beneficent god, made much of by the military—their God of War, and in certain provinces, the God of Literature. Merchants also revered him. Above all he exemplified selflessness, integrity, loyalty and wisdom.

On the first day of the New Year most people from the city or countryside, visit a temple to pray for good fortune and blessings. Each one goes with a different wish, but all fervently hope that their own will be fulfilled. However, there are some who do not believe in such things. That little orphan boy from the T'ao clan for instance, the one with the pockmarked face, nicknamed Little Pock Face (but he did not mind it)—he never had any good fortune or blessings, nor did he seek any. He just happened to be loitering that early New Year's morning in the Kuan Ti Temple. Someone was coming in to offer New Year gifts and pray. Little Pock Face was merely curious to see what would happen, so he hid behind the big statue of Kuan Ti.

That was how he happened to see Dr. Li, owner of an herb shop in town arrive carrying large *joss sticks,* tea and cakes, and yellow paper. (All the wishes of a supplicant are written on yellow paper and burned in the presence of the god to whom the petition is made.) Placing the tea and cakes on the altar, he lit the joss, kotowed and knelt to pray. "I am the herbalist, Dr. Li," he said. "I have come especially to pay you respect for the New Year. O Living Buddha, please cast a spell so there is an epidemic this year; then I'll be very busy and have many patients. I promise to return next year in the early morning and bring tribute to repay you for your blessings!"

After he left Little Pock Face saw a Taoist priest named Wang come in. He too offered incense, lit some candles, kotowed and also knelt to pray, "O Reverend Kuan Ti, my old Buddha in Heaven, I beg you to bless my family," he implored. "But please spread disease on my fellow beings so I'll be very busy with calls to say prayers for the dead. When I return next year on this very morning I promise to offer you a lantern that will be lit all year round, and burn *joss sticks* the year round too!" After his vow, he also left.

Soon the proprietor of a coffin shop, a fat fellow with a big head, nicknamed Fatty Wu, came in. He began his prayers by saying, "I had a bad year last year. There wasn't much business so I still have a big quantity of merchandise stored in my shop. Please Old Buddha, with your blessings enable me to sell all my coffins this year. By harvest time I promise to build a new temple for you!"

After he left some village farmers came in. They came simply to offer New Year greetings. They had no gifts, but when they kotowed they prayed, "Old Buddha, grant us blessings for a good year, suitable wind, enough rain and a bountiful harvest, and good health for men and animals. We promise to bring offerings, *joss sticks* and candles next year to repay you and show our gratitude!"

Little Pock Face heard everything clearly; besides, he knew all these people, especially the herbalist, Li and Fatty Wu. When the orphan was a small boy begging for food at their doorsteps, he recalled how they beat him and kicked him out. He was now eighteen years old, and as he listened to their supplications, he recalled his hate for them "They are really intolerable," he thought to himself. "There must be some way to punish them."

The first thing he did was go to Fatty Wu's store and call out, "The son of the herbalist, Dr. Li, who lives up the street, had a fit after the New Year dinner last night! By daybreak his son was dead. Li sent me here. Do you have a coffin on hand? I must go back to let him know. The doctor himself will be here soon."

"Yes, yes, we do. Please come in," the coffin proprietor said with a beaming smile.

In the past when Little Pock Face came to beg, not only would Fatty Wu heap abuses on him, he always slammed the door in his face. But now he was suddenly so courteous, asking the young fellow in, even offering him tea and tobacco!

Little Pock Face then hurried to the herbalist shop to see Dr. Li, and said, "The coffin proprietor's wife suddenly became ill this morning. She is in a serious condition, and purposely sent me to ask you to look at her immediately."

The herbalist became very excited and called his daughter to help wrap the herbs. His wife sitting nearby remarked, "Daughter, please be quick. People are waiting. Today is the first of the year; such good luck augurs well for the rest of the year."

Meanwhile the herbalist mumbled to himself, "That was a mighty good prayer I offered Buddha," and hastily departed with Little Pock Face who took him to the front door of the coffin proprietor's store.

"Please doctor," Little Pock Face said, "old proprietor Wu is waiting for you inside. Please go in." Little Pock Face then disappeared and went on his way to the Taoist priest.

Proprietor Wu happened to see the herbalist enter so he quickly went to usher his visitor to the guest room where he placed New Year candies on the table, and offered tea and tobacco. The two exchanged New Year greetings, and after a while Fatty Wu stood up and asked Dr. Li, "Will you come with me to have a look?"

The doctor followed saying, "Very good, very good— *ch'ing, ch'ing* (please, please).

Fatty Wu then led Dr. Li to the place where the coffins were stored and said, "Please make your own choice. When you decide, the price can be talked about later."

The herbalist was puzzled, and cutting short any further conversation, he asked, "Isn't your wife very sick? Why bring me to look at coffins?"

"What bad luck to say such things on the first day of the year!" Fatty Wu thought almost losing his temper. But he cooled down because of the prospective business and merely said, "There's no sickness in my house. But you sent a messenger to tell me that your son died of sudden illness. Haven't you come to buy a coffin?"

Hearing this infuriated Dr. Li who began to curse. Curses were hurled back and forth until the argument became increasingly heated.

Meanwhile Little Pock Face had reached the place where the Taoist priest lived. "The coffin proprietor's son died of sudden sickness!" the youth exclaimed. "The body is already in the coffin. But since it's New Year's day with no helper around, I was asked to fetch you to say prayers for his son. The quicker you get there the better."

After hearing the news, the priest stopped eating his noon-day meal, gave up the pleasure of his wine cup, and hurried along with his bell and prayer book in hand.

When Taoist Wang arrived the two men were still engaged in a heated argument. Both immediately asked him to pass judgment. But not waiting for them to finish their explanation, Taoist Wang said, "What are you arguing about on New Year's day?! Let matters be. Wu's son is already dead. I have come to offer prayers for the dead . . ."

Fatty Wu almost burst with anger. Without waiting for any further questions he raised his fist aiming at the priest. No time for questions! The priest replied by thrusting his own fist at Fatty Wu. The three men thereupon began to pummel one another in earnest.

Hearing the brawl, the son, daughter and wife of Fatty Wu, rushed out to help him. They fought ferociously inside the house and then outside on the road. Many people were attracted by the commotion and gathered to watch. Although bruised and injured, none would stop fighting until some neighbors forcibly parted them, and tried to find out what had started such a terrible fight to begin with.

"There he is!" the three shouted almost simultaneously as they spotted Little Pock Face among the crowd. "He is the trouble maker!" they screamed rushing toward him with raised fists.

But Little Pock Face boldly stood his ground and with chest puffed out, told the crowd everything he had heard while lingering in the temple. "So! What do you want?" he demanded of the three men, "I purposely did this to show you for what you are. I wanted everyone to know how despicable you truly are!"

With that, the people burst out laughing and started to clap. "A good fight!" they exclaimed, "A good fight!"

The three men were speechless, hung their heads in shame and went home without uttering a word.

# The Beggar Scholar

*A Han Folktale*

In ancient times scholars crowded the examination halls to pass a test on the classics, history, martial arts and so forth. Those who succeeded were awarded important official posts. Power, influence, wealth and fame followed as a result. The preparation was arduous, and young scholars often went to an isolated place such as an abandoned temple or an ancient ruin to concentrate on their studies. During their confinement many strange happenings occurred, sometimes because of mental imbalance, lack of nourishment, cold or other deprivation. Tales about ghosts, foxes, fairies or supernatural phenomena were inspired by the experiences of the scholars. Real or imaginary, the tales formed an inexhaustible reservoir for storytellers. The public examination system was abolished after the Republic was founded only sixty-four years ago.

This folktale portrayed the exalted status of the scholar, his ambition to achieve a governmental post, and the ingratitude, avarice and obsequious nature of one scholar in particular who would stoop to anything to acquire a coveted official position.

In a district near Nanking there was once a beggar named Chang who lived with his daughter in a broken-down hut. One day the whole air was thick with snow and a cruel northwind howled. In spite of that Chang went out as usual to beg while his daughter remained home. Looking out to see how bad the storm was, she was startled to see a dying man lying nearby. Pulling herself together, she ventured outside to look more closely. She noticed that his lips were quivering, and his delicate features were those of a scholar. Moreover, he was still breathing. So with all the strength that she could muster, she dragged him into the hut. She started a fire, and cooked some ginger broth to revive him.

After a time he recovered and found that he was no longer lying in the snow, but a beautiful young woman was taking care of him. "*Ee-e*, how could I have got here!" he cried out. "I was frozen to death. Ah, you have saved my life. I'll be eternally grateful to you."

"No need to thank me," she replied very simply. "Better drink some more broth quickly—you're still cold."

While he was sipping the broth, her father returned and his daughter explained what had happened.

"What is your name? Whatever were you doing out in such a snowstorm?" he anxiously questioned the young man.

"Old uncle, my name is Mo Kwei. I'm an orphan from

a poor family. When my parents were alive, I studied the classics, but now I have to beg for a living. This heavy snow was so unexpected. With so little clothing and the bitterly cold wind, I lost control of myself and fell down. If not for your daughter, I would have perished from the cold and hunger. I'll never forget her kindness."

Old beggar Chang felt very sorry for him. Then noting his fine features, the old man said, "Since you don't have any home, you can stay with us."

Thereupon Mo Kwei stayed in the old ramshackle hut and helped however he could. After a few months the daughter and young man fell in love with each other, and the father consented to their marriage.

It happened that there was to be a public examination that year. With his wife's encouragement, he resumed his studies and worked hard to prepare for his dream. He passed successfully, and so the old father-in-law also helped by giving him money for travel to the capital to participate in the final imperial examination. He again passed, being placed first. He was certainly fortunate!

With these happy tidings Mo Kwei returned to take his family to the capital. He hired a large boat and began the journey. In the beginning the three people were happy. But one night Mo Kwei began to speculate on the chances of rising more quickly in the official world, and thought, "Since I'm an important official, it is most inappropriate to have a wife who is only a beggar's daughter." After deliberating for some time he made up his mind and called to his wife, "Gracious Lady," (which was the typical way for an official to address his wife. Her own name was never used) "see how bright the moon is! Will you please come to the front of the boat to enjoy it?"

Hearing her husband call, she hurried to the front of the boat. While they were enjoying the beauty of the river scene, Mo Kwei gave her a big push, and then cried out, "A calamity! Father-in-law!" Mo Kwei pretended to be alarmed and began to stutter, "She, she fell, fell into the river."

The old father rushed to the front and bent low trying to reach his daughter. Now Mo Kwei had already planned his next move, and with all his force, shoved the old man into the water also.

"It is hopeless to save them. Maybe we can think of a way later. Just row on," Mo Kwei said to the boatmen.

So the boat went on. With a strong wind and swift current, he was able to reach the capital in a few days.

Within a month after assuming his post, a matchmaker approached Mo Kwei to say that the Minister of Justice would like to have him as a son-in-law. "Ah! A minister's daughter for my wife," Mo Kwei thought quite pleased. He readily agreed and a date was set for the marriage.

On the night of the ceremony, Mo Kwei happily entered the marriage chamber where his new wife awaited him. Eager to see her he walked toward the bride and lifted the red silk veil covering her face. He lowered his head to look at her, but jumped back after a glance, and called out "Ghost! Ghost!" He was really terrified.

The Minister of Justice and old beggar Chang entered the room. Seeing his previous father-in-law, Mo Kwei realized that the bride was none other than his own wife. Knowing it was useless to keep the secret any longer he knelt before the minister.

"Why should you kneel in front of me?" the minister asked feigning ignorance.

"It is because I, a little fellow, lost my sanity and foolishly committed a crime. I was without compassion; I had no conscience."

"Aha—so that is your plea. I can't make any final judgment. I'll have to present your case to the emperor tomorrow."

"Honorable Sir, please forgive me this time. I have worked so hard to become a scholar, studying by the light of a window in a cold room for over ten years." Tears streamed down his face for he knew that not only his official post would be lost, but his life.

"A heartless person like you doesn't deserve to live," the minister angrily replied. "If my boat hadn't been following behind yours and my boatman hadn't noticed the floating bodies and rescued them, you would have succeeded in killing both father and daughter. And what a death! How innocent they are! You became a high official but you have an evil heart. You brought harm to the very people who saved your life. Where is your conscience? You want to marry the adopted daughter of a minister, but discard a beggar's daughter. You are a rascal without character, greedy for power and fame. Even after ten years studying the rules of behavior toward the family, friends, and the sovereign, you can commit such a crime! Huh," he said with scorn as he walked out with old beggar Chang.

Turning to his wife, the young scholar humbly pleaded, "O Gracious Lady, please forgive me."

"Who is your Gracious Lady? Maid, hurry, bring me three wooden sticks." With that she and the two servants began to beat him severely.

"*E-ya*, Gracious Lady, I'm dying from pain! Be merciful!" he cried.

Beggar Chang entered and seeing Mo Kwei's condition, took pity on him. He placed his son-in-law on a bench and gave him a cup of tea. Yet he could not help scolding him and said, "You look like a decent person. Who would ever suspect you had no heart? You repaid gratitude with malice and wanted to destroy us both. You became an official but your post actually depended on my money from begging. Without it, you would still be a beggar."

"Father-in-law, have pity on me; save the life of your son-in-law," he pleaded.

The old man became sympathetic and spoke to the minister who intended to have the scholar punished. After a time the minister agreed because the young scholar really seemed to regret what he had done. Only Mo Kwei's wife remained adamant.

Mo Kwei prostrated himself before her imploring forgiveness. Then his wife thought, "Since I saved his life once before, why should I insist on destroying him now?" So in turn, she too become compassionate and pardoned her husband.

Mo Kwei became an unusually good, upright person and thereafter lived quite happily with his family.

# *Iron Crutch Li and Gold Finger Wang*

*A Han Folktale*

Many folktales were told about Lao-tze, who recorded his philosophy in *the Tao Te Ching* (The Way and Virtuous Path of Tao) and his disciples. His philosophy embraced all mankind but was primarily directed toward the Chou Dynasty vassals who strove to acquire the hegemony by any means, foul or fair, and the inept, degenerate sovereign who was losing control over the kingdom and as a result the cruel, interminable wars, corruption and chaos brought poverty and suffering to the common people.

The most popular ones revolved around a group of Eight Immortals. Some of the eight were historic personages of the T'ang Dynasty; some were added during or after the Sung Dynasty. Iron Crutch Li was supposedly one of Lao-tze's friends. Like the others, he attained spiritual perfection and therefore became an Immortal. Each Immortal possessed a special magical power. Li had the gourd. "What potent medicine from your gourd are you selling this time?" was a popular saying that meant, "Now what are you up to?"

As one of Lao-tze's followers, Iron Crutch Li found the greed, lust and guile of Gold Finger Wang intolerable. In this folktale, Wang was portrayed as the little man unable to cope with affluence. The magic golden tip on his finger was too much for him, and like many of his fellow beings, instead of using power and wealth for a good purpose, he abused the privilege until it was taken away.

There was a little village situated on the high plains north of the River Wei. In this village dwelt a young man named Wang. He was accustomed to extravagant living although he had already squandered his father's wealth. Besides, his father was no longer living to help or spoil him anymore. But he had been brought up amidst wealth. How then could he labor like the others from morning as the sun rose in the east until evening when the sun set in the west? It would bring shame on his ancestors to go into the fields and work. Thus the few remaining plots of farmland were overgrown with long grass. The neighbors despised him, and behind his back, called him Rusty Iron Lock. (An iron lock was used only to safeguard money; hence the nickname implied Wang's uselessness.)

"The day will come when my good fortune will reverse things," Wang constantly said, "I won't be a man if I don't reestablish the affluence of my ancestors."

One autumn noon Wang was having a nap. Just as he was enjoying a dream, the noisy chirping of a magpie awakened him. "Loathsome bird!" he shouted angrily and went back to sleep again.

"Wang! Wang!" the magpie persisted. "Wake up! Hurry! The Eight Immortals will soon be coming!"

"Never heard of a magpie speaking human language," he mumbled half-conscious and drifted off to sleep again, thinking he was still dreaming.

After a while the magpie called excitedly, "Wang! Wang! Hurry! Hurry! Hurry! The Eight Immortals are coming this way now!"

This time Wang was fully awake. Opening his eyes wide, he poked his head out the window. Some people were approaching from the west—each one dressed in very strange attire. He counted eight of them. "That girl must be the Immortal, Maiden Ho," he thought to himself. "The one on the back of a hairy donkey must be the Immortal, Chang. The one at the very end limping with the support of an iron crutch must be the Immortal, Li! Right! Right! They are the Eight Immortals!" he exclaimed. All of a sudden he realized that he was seeing a miracle. He hastily put on his clothing, very carefully

wrapped the title deed of his ancestors' remaining farmland and a few of his favorite articles in a bundle, and
rushed from his house. He followed closely behind Iron
Crutch Li.

None of the Eight Immortals paid any attention to
him. Iron Crutch Li who was right in front of him, did
not even turn his head around. But Wang stuck around
anyway and followed them until they reached the bank of
the River Wei. It happened that the river had risen to a
great height and the foaming water and swift current

were rushing down toward the east. It was so wide, even the other side of the bank was not visible.

"Excellent water! Today everyone of us will tread on the white foam to cross the river. The one who spoils the pattern of the current will be the host when we reach Chung-nan Shan." (A legendary mountain where all the Immortals assembled. *Chung-nan* means extreme south; *shan*, mountain.)

"Well said! But how about that fellow following us?" Iron Crutch Li suddenly asked without even turning his head as if he already knew what was in Wang's mind.

"It all depends on whether he can attain the Way. If he does, bring him across; if not, talk about it later."

"If you want to follow us crossing the river, it isn't difficult," Iron Crutch Li confided as he turned his head. "Only promise three things," he said as he stretched his three fingers.

Immediately, Wang replied, "Please bring me across the river and help me to become an Immortal. I'll promise even thirty things, that I swear."

"Well then, first of all no distractions. You must only look ahead or you'll drown."

"I'll do as you say. I will, I will."

"The second thing, throw your possessions into the river, and don't feel bad about it or regret it."

Of course Wang was reluctant because this meant his ancestors' title deed had to be discarded, and he needed that to accumulate money. However, through his mind flashed the thought, "If I become an Immortal, I can recover the title deed from the riverbed." So he agreed and instantly threw the bundle near the riverbank.

"The third point," continued Iron Crutch Li, "Immortals don't eat cooked human food. I have here a half bowl of enchanted soup, primarily to wash away the refuse from your body, but it will also serve as your meal.

You may take it." Li then removed the big gourd from his shoulder.

Thinking that the enchanted soup must be very tasty, Wang replied with alacrity, "I'll drink it! I'll drink it!"

"Pick up a squash leaf and use it as a cup," Li commanded as he opened the lid of his gourd.

Fellow Wang immediately obeyed. Wiping the dust off the leaf with his dress, he folded it between his hands to make a concave cup. Iron Crutch Li very carefully poured some liquid, drop by drop.

"This must be the enchanted juice," Wang thought. "But it looks black and dirty. It must be scores of years old!" A queer, offensive smell irritated his nose. There were little worm-like things wriggling in the juice! Fellow Wang almost threw up at the sight of it. Without realizing, he closed his eyes, drew back and cried, *"E-ya!* Can this be drunk?"

Iron Crutch Li's face dropped a little as he asked, "You can't drink it? Very well, let me have it." He took the squash leaf out of Wang's hand and swooped the contents into his mouth like eating noodles. Then stuffing the leaf into his garment, Li said, "Let me tell you—this is the enchanted juice given to me by the Fairy Queen Mother of the Western Heavens. You acted as though I gave you something bad that couldn't be swallowed. Go back. I have to cross the river."

"O, good fairy! Have mercy on me!" Fellow Wang cried as he knelt down, kotowed and begged.

"Get up! You can't attain the Way. You don't have the willpower to suffer hardship. You aren't qualified to dwell in Paradise. I pity you for having followed us half the day so I'll give you the squash leaf. It will bring you good luck provided you are good to your neighbors and don't commit any misdeed. See you later." With that Li threw the squash leaf into Wang's lap, stepped into the river, and floated toward the other Immortals.

Fellow Wang saw the Eight Immortals heading south, treading the waves just like walking on a smooth road. He deeply regretted not having the determination to drink the juice. Nothing could be done now except pick up the squash leaf. For a long time he patiently scraped with his forefinger to get whatever was still on the leaf. It amounted to only one drop. So he started to lick it slowly. 'Ah-ya! Strange!' Like magic he instantly felt a sense of warmth and well-being all over, and smelled an ethereal fragrance like the ginseng fruit. He kept on licking the leaf until it was no longer sweet but bitter. Only then did he reluctantly throw it away. At that moment he noticed the first two joints of his forefinger had turned yellow and shiny as gold!

"That must be from scraping the squash leaf!" he exclaimed. "This gold finger should make me rich!" He was so elated, and took care to protect his finger by placing it in his mouth. At last he recovered his bundle near the riverbank and returned home, feeling very satisfied.

One spring a serious epidemic of diptheria spread throughout his village. Wang was not affected, but those who were  succumbed to the disease. Then he told his neighbors about his enchanted finger and people named him Gold-finger Wang for as soon as anybody sucked it, they were cured! Multitudes came to him for help, and all were cured. He acted as a good neighbor to each villager.

But after a time he began to deliberate and thought it opportune to take advantage of the epidemic, and so recover his ancestors' wealth. For a patient's first visit, he charged an exorbitant fee and gave it the special name of "the opening gift." People had to mortgage their property or quite often sell it to him if they wished to be saved.

Wang satisfied his conscience by saying, "It's my destiny to become richer than my neighbors. If they have to suffer, that's heaven's wish. After all, didn't the Immortal, Li, give me the gold finger and after that create an epidemic?"

Gold-finger Wang's nails are really long!" people whispered. "With a single scratch he can destroy a whole family."

After Wang had accumulated wealth like his ancestors, he did not even want to see poor people, and became a specialist for the wealthy only. What mischief he created! What harm he did! Conniving with the influential or powerful ones, he behaved like a real scoundrel.

One day an old man with a long, white beard in a large sedan chair borne by eight husky attendants arrived at his home. Observing their arrival, Wang thought to himself, "That old man must be a very high official," and he immediately began to scheme, "here is my chance to get an official post." Thereupon he examined the old man and then very respectfully stretched out his hand and placed his gold finger into the old man's mouth.

But then a most unexpected thing occurred—the old man squinted his eyes and bit off the gold finger! "Do you recognize me?" he shouted in a fierce voice. "I can't allow this benevolent object to be used as an instrument to destroy people!"

Fellow Wang rolled on the ground in severe pain. "Whose voice was that?" he thought only half-conscious. Very vaguely he recalled hearing it before. "That was it! Iron Crutch Li was speaking!"

In a short time Wang passed away and the village was later known as the Golden-finger Village.

# The Will

*A Han Folktale*

In ancient times worship of heaven, earth, and the ancestors was very important. The desire for male posterity arose from the practice of ancestral worship whereby the male head of a family performed the rituals. When he died, the eldest son, or a male next of kin, took his place. If there was only a married daughter, her husband assumed this responsibility and was treated like a son, if he seemed devoted to the family. In that case, property, money or worldly goods, were bequeathed to him. There was much scheming and many tragic incidents as a result.

Although the baby in this story was called *Tai* (Big) as the eldest, his middle name *Fai* (Not, a negative), indicated that he was physically small. A Chinese had a number of names besides the given name: a milk name—as an infant; a school name—on first attending school; another on reaching manhood; one for scholarship; a professional name; a retirement name, etc.

Practicing law became a modern profession only after lengthy contact with the West. Prior to that, a magistrate controlled law and order. Some were notorious for being corrupt and lacking in wisdom; others were upright and sagacious, as in this tale. The play on words and elimination of punctuation in the old man's will, enabled the son-in-law to interpret it in his favor. The astute magistrate prevented what would have been a miscarriage of justice.

There was once a rich man, over seventy years of age, living in Ch'angchow. He had only a daughter, who helped manage his affairs. After she married, her husband managed the old man's properties. At first, his son-in-law took good care of the old man, but his attitude gradually changed to indifference. At times, he treated the old man very badly.

One day, old man Chiang thought to himself, "After all, a son-in-law is an outsider. Besides, he has his own parents to consider. Naturally, he would be inclined to protect the interests of his immediate family above all. Although I'm elderly, I'm still strong. Why not marry a second time? I might have a son, and in that case, the Chiang lineage would be continued."

A matchmaker was sent to a family in a nearby village. They consented to the marriage and a wedding was subsequently arranged. Shortly afterwards, his wife actually bore a baby boy. The old man's daughter and his son-in-law were very upset. But after all, what could they do? Old Chiang was truly a happy man.

A big celebration was held according to custom when the child was one month and given a name. He was named Chiang Tai Fei (Chiang Big Not), but was known by his milk name, Chiang Tai (Chiang Big or the eldest son of Chiang).

Time passed quickly, and after two years, old Chiang became seriously ill. Knowing that his end was near, he wrote two wills. The first was given privately to his wife, and he coached her thus: "I realize that my son-in-law is lacking in filial devotion. With my ancestors' blessings, you, my wife, gave me a son thereby ensuring the continuity of the Chiang family. I'm leaving my property entirely to you. However, our son is only three years old, (as soon as a baby was born, he was considered a year old) and since you're an illiterate woman, I'm afraid that my son-in-law will take advantage of you. It may seem as though my properties are being given to him— but wait until our son comes of age. Then go immediately to a righteous magistrate, declare your legal status and claim the properties. Always remember the child's given name is Chiang Big Not. That is of utmost importance."

She carefully hid the will, and then the old man had his son-in-law called to his deathbed, to give him a will.

53

"I've treated you well," he said. "Hereafter, you must look after your mother-in-law and her baby son. Don't make any trouble for them. Promise me that so I'll be able to die in peace."

"Yes, Yes," the son-in-law said respectfully, taking the will. But since character writing has no system of capitalization and Old Chiang had omitted punctuation, the son-in-law interpreted the will according to his own wishful thinking, and read "Chiang big—not my son— to whom all property belongs son-in-law—outsider forbidden inheritance." This pleased him, and for a time he was most considerate of his mother-in-law and the child. But gradually he neglected them.

The years quickly elapsed and the young boy was now of age. The mother remembered her husband's last words and the will, so she brought her son with the will to a righteous magistrate to claim the properties.

The son-in-law was not worried over the contest of the old man's will because he believed that he possessed the will, and he promptly presented it to the magistrate. The handwriting was indisputably the old man's. Yet the neighbors said that the will was unfair since the old man had written it when very ill, already not in control of his faculties. Nonetheless, it was a legal document, so the magistrate scrutinized it without saying a word, and did likewise with the will presented by the second wife. After examining them both, and hearing the neighbors' explanations, he felt that something was wrong with the son-in-law's will, and pondered the matter for some time.

"What is the name of your father-in-law's son?" he asked the son-in-law.

"Chiang Big," he answered. "Everyone knows him by that name and calls him that."

"What is the name of your son," the magistrate asked the mother.

"His name is Chiang Big Not. Chiang Big is his milk name."

"Have you heard what was said? Is this statement correct?" he asked the son-in-law.

The son-in-law was thinking that everybody called the baby by the milk name of Chiang Big but his true given name was Chiang Big Not. So he nodded in agreement.

With that, the magistrate openly declared before the son-in-law, the daughter, the mother, all the relatives and neighbors present, "Old man Chiang was very clever. If the will had not been written in this manner, all the property would belong to his son-in-law. Something unfortunate might even have happened to the mother and son. This will was purposely written without punctuation. Thereupon he gave the proper punctuation to the will and officially declared it in order. "A given name must be used in all legal documents." Then he read aloud, "Chiang Big Not, my son to whom all properties belong; son-in-law, outsider, forbidden inheritance." The hidden meaning was thus revealed.

Everyone praised the fairness of the magistrate, and the wisdom of old Chiang.

# Buddhistic Prayer

*A Han Folktale*

The first day of each month and the fifteenth (the first full moon) a Buddhist devotee of the sect known as the Ch'ing T'u (Pure Land), abstained from all meat, and either wearing beads or fingering them, repeated the Buddhist incantation, *O Mi To Fu.* As in this folktale, elderly people often spent a great deal of time repeating the prayer. But little else was required by the faith such as meditation, study of sutras or attendance at a temple for the soul to go to Paradise when a person died. Hence this particular sect was most popular among the laity.

⌂ ⌂ ⌂

There was once an elderly couple, natives of Kiangsi Province. A-yin, the old man, was learned but did not believe in religion. On the other hand, his wife, Siu-chiu, was a devout follower of Buddhism. The first thing she did on arising early each morning, was to burn incense and thereafter repeat the Buddhist incantation '*O Mi To Fu, O Mi To Fu . . . .*' In fact, she neglected everything else.

A-yin bore this with remarkable fortitude, but became really tired of hearing her chant the livelong day and implored her to stop. Yet she continued from early morning till late at night as though she had never even heard him. He did not like the neighbors to hear him argue with her so he patiently endured it. In spite of that, he never gave up trying to think of a way to silence her.

At last one day, the old man found a way and this is what he did: from early morning onward he called out his wife's own name: "my Siu-chiu, my Siu-chiu . . . ."

He kept on calling her until she found it so intolerable

she became exasperated and said, "Why do you keep on making noises by calling my name? You tedious thing!"

"I have called your name only a few times yet you are already angry," he calmly replied. "How many times do you call O Mi To Fu? A thousandfold each day! Do you think that Buddha isn't tired of hearing you?"

Thereafter, although she remained a faithful adherent to Buddhism in all respects, Siu-chiu ceased her chanting.

# The Clever Wife

*A Han Folktale*

There were quite a few Han folktales about a clever woman whereas the man was often a dullard, or at least no match for her. China was predominantly a man's world, yet there were times when a woman was the actual power behind the throne; occasionally she was the sovereign. As a wife, mother or mother-in-law, she frequently exerted a powerful influence on the family. Even as a daughter, she could be forceful. One such instance was the famed heroine, Mu Lan. Unusually skillful and clever in swordsmanship, she went to war instead of her sick father, who, having no son, had trained her since childhood in the martial arts. And Hsi Shih, a woman of rare beauty, helped to bring about the downfall of a kingdom by concealing her cleverness with feminine wiles. It is interesting to see how the magistrate in this story thought he was clever, but how the woman outwitted him.

There was a man from Chekiang Province who married a very clever woman. She was exceptionally capable and solved all their problems, no matter how difficult. Thus they gradually became prosperous. He was so happy, to please his wife as well as glorify her, he wrote a poem on red paper and posted it on his front door (as was the custom for announcements such as marriage, birth, etc., red paper being the color symbolic of happiness).

*Which family can compare with mine?*
*Neither help nor favors*
*Need I beg from mankind.*

One day a magistrate happened to pass their front entrance, and noticed the poem. "Who in all the world would be that proud and boastful?" he wondered. On his return to the magistracy, he decided to send two petty officials to fetch the master of the house.

*"Ai-ya,* what have I done? What's wrong? Something serious I'm sure," he told his wife when he learned of the summons.

But after only a moment's thought, his wife realized that it must have something to do with the poem on their door. "You were in such high spirits when you wrote the poem. Since it has already created trouble, just follow the officers. Luckily, it's only a trivial matter. If there are any difficulties, we can talk about them later."

He accompanied the officers and appeared before the magistrate who said, "The poem on your front door expressed great arrogance. It seems that you alone can accomplish all things. Now then, I'll ask you to do three things: the first is to weave a cloth as long as the road; the second, to brew a quantity of wine as big as the ocean; and the third, to raise a pig as heavy as the mountain. If you can accomplish these, I'll pardon you. But if you fail, don't blame me for giving you severe punishment," the magistrate warned, intent on giving the fellow a lesson to remember.

'All this trouble! *Ai-ya,* it's my own fault,' he thought as he bowed low and left. He was very glum as he trod homeward to relate everything to his clever wife.

"Don't be a fool," she laughed. "Why should you be so afraid? Tomorrow you can report to the magistrate."

"How can I possibly go back to him?" he asked her.

"Just reply that you will be able to accomplish what he wants."

"But how?"

"You only have to bring a ruler, a measuring bowl for rice and a kitchen scale. When you see the magistrate, just say . . . ", she whispered in his ear. "I'm sure he won't make any trouble for us."

After listening to what his wife had whispered, he went to the magistrate and said, "I'll be able to carry out all of the three things, you asked. But first, will Your Honor please use this ruler to measure the road so that I can know how long to weave the cloth; and I must ask Your Honor to measure the quantity of water in the ocean by using this standard measuring bowl so that I can brew the wine accordingly; and again, please Your Honor, use this scale to weigh the mountain so that I can raise a pig as heavy as the mountain."

As he was talking he gave the ruler, bowl and kitchen scale to the magistrate who accepted them in silence.

"What an oaf this man is! How could such a simple, foolish-looking fellow have figured that out?" he wondered. So he asked in a soft, low voice, "Confidentially, who taught you the answers?"

"It was my wife's good counsel," the man answered truthfully.

The magistrate nodded and said, "You are indeed fortunate to have such a clever wife. I'm not going to bother you any further."

# The Reward from a Sparrow

*A Han Folktale*

For the most part, a domestic dwelling formerly had a roof of pan and roll clay tiles. Once a year, a swallow might build a nest under the eave, which was welcomed as a favorable omen. But the little sparrow fat from eating grains in a field or courtyard, frequently built under the roof tiles in a crevice or any opening. It was a constant visitor, flying in and out of a house at any time.

As a part of the daily scene, the common sparrow in this folktale, brought the message of Buddhist teachings that good was rewarded and evil punished. But *Kung Kung* (which means granduncle) one of the minor gods in the Chinese pantheon, in charge of each district, watched over the daily happenings, reported to the God of Heaven, and dispensed the fitting reward or punishment. Great care was taken to pay homage to these gods. There were special days to pay respect, the New Year being the most important when colorful portraits of the Kitchen God, the Earth God, and the Door God and such, were posted on the main entrance of a house or within the home. Incense and *joss sticks* were burned, candles lit, and offerings of food were placed on an altar.

There was once a little sparrow that made several valiant attempts to fly, but each time fell to earth. A kind, young woman saw it limp along and exclaimed,"Ai-ya, it must have a broken foot!" She took it home, applied some healing herbs, bound the foot, and fed the bird until it had fully recovered. Within a few days, the sparrow flew away. But not long after, it returned with a watermelon seed in its beak that it dropped into the woman's lap. Since it was only a watermelon seed, she threw it into her courtyard. But the next spring, the seed

61

grew into a vine and by summertime there was a big watermelon.

One day, she invited many relatives and friends to celebrate her birthday. At the end of the meal, she took the ripened melon from her garden to share with her guests. But when she opened it, everyone was astonished—the melon was filled with seeds of gold! Who would have expected such a thing from the tiny seed?

"A miracle!" they exclaimed. "Tell us about it," they begged in a hushed voice. And being an honest person, she told them what had happened. They listened in rapt attention, and all were happy for her good luck. But one envious woman memorized every detail for she had secretly decided to try her own luck.

On her return, she caught a little sparrow, purposely broke its foot, then applied some herbs, bandaged its foot, and fed the pitiful bird exactly as the kind woman had done. Within a few days, the sparrow recovered and flew away. The next day, it came back and dropped a watermelon seed into her lap whereupon she exclaimed, "Ah, the bird is rewarding me!" She hurriedly went to plant the seed. And that spring there was a vine, and by summertime, a big watermelon.

She too chose a lucky day, and pretending it was her birthday, ordered wine, meat and other choice food to entertain her relatives and friends. But when she opened the melon—goodness! Everyone was astonished to see a kung kung with silvery white hair, and a long flowing beard jump out! Who would have expected such a thing from a tiny seed? He extended his arm, gave the woman two resounding slaps on each cheek and then disappeared.

# The Fate of the Trouble-Maker

*A Han Folktale*

Long, long ago in what is now China, the tribespeople worshipped thunder, lightning, fire, wind or rain, and all animals and birds. They believed that each had a spirit that was related to people. Every clan chose a particular natural element, an animal or a bird as a namesake, and the entire tribe bore the name that stood as its emblem and protector. These beliefs and practices are rendered in Chinese as *T'u-t'eng*, meaning Totem. Totem had religious significance.

Related to this totemic practice was the custom of assigning an animal as the ruler of a year. There was a belief that the spirit of one animal controlled each person the year he was born. There were twelve animals designating the months of the year and each had a special significance. Initially, these animals showed a close affinity with the astrological symbolism of the Sumerians and Hebrews. But in the course of time, the animals and symbolic meanings changed considerably. When people were hunters, activities took place in the autumn, and festivals marked the New Year after the hunt. The cock was then the symbol. When hunting was displaced by farming, the year began at the vernal equinox, and the ox or buffalo (according to the region) became a symbol and chief of the animals. Finally legend relates that all the animals of the forest met to decide who was to be the leader, and the mouse was unanimously chosen because of its superior wisdom. The mouse has remained the first animal in the lunar cycle of twelve animals, followed by the buffalo or ox, then the tiger, rabbit, heavenly dragon, snake, horse, ram, monkey, cock, dog and lastly the pig. At no time was the fox included in the group of creatures. It has always been regarded as a supernatural creature that could change itself into a human being, generally a beautiful woman who caused misery or unhappiness to the person she became attached to. Its spirit was evil, and the fox symbolized a schemer, a trouble-maker as in this folktale.

Among the high mountains, swift rivers and dense forests in Kwangsi Province there once lived an old tigress with her cub. Because of her age she was almost incapaple of going to hunt. But luckily one day a herd of buffalos came near her cave and an old mother buffalo was trailing behind with her little one.

"At last a chance to have a banquet," the old tigress purred as she attacked the buffalo who was far too old to run away.

Not having eaten for many days, the hungry tigress devoured the buffalo almost whole, stuffing herself until she could not even stand up. Afterward the tigress rolled in agony. But before she finally died, she mumbled to her little one, "This is my end. After my death, you must be a good friend to the little buffalo. Never fight over food or be greedy, and always protect each other. Remember!"

The little tiger obeyed his mother's wishes and treated the young buffalo very well, guarding her at all times. They lived together, played and slept together just as though they were of the same family. No other tiger ever bothered the little buffalo because she was the cub's friend. At the same time no other buffalo ever dared approach her because she was with the tiger. She became so accustomed to living with the tiger that she never even thought of herself as a buffalo.

"They are such good friends," a jealous fox observed one day. "I must separate them no matter how good they are to each other. After all, a tiger and a buffalo can't live together forever."

So one day when the little tiger was eating some deer's meat, the cunning fox approached, and said respectfully, "Oh Tiger King, I can see that your precious life will be threatened soon by a calamity. Your good friend, the little buffalo, is scheming to kill you to avenge her mother's death. You must be very careful."

The little tiger simply could not believe the fox, and kept thinking, "We have been together since babyhood and always good friends. However, humm, since the fox said so, let me ask him what made him say this." Thereupon he asked the fox, "How do you know it will happen?"

"King Tiger," the fox replied, "if you don't believe me, I can prove it. Just go ahead and find the buffalo. If you see her with her head lowered, her horns pointing toward you, her tail flapping under her belly, and snorting, these are the signals that she intends to kill you. Don't hesitate to pounce on her and bite her to death."

After hearing this, the cub was actually convinced.

At the same time the fox ran to the little buffalo and said, "Oh you poor little buffalo, I know the tiger is going to kill you. Are you going to be content with the same fate as your mother?"

The little buffalo was scared by these ill-tidings, and asked the fox what to do.

"When the tiger comes near you," the cunning fox replied, "lower your head, point your horns toward him, flap your tail on your belly and snort. Prepare to charge in order to defend yourself."

Truly, just as the fox had planned, one day this happened. Without an exchange of a single word, both engaged in a serious fight. Once good old friends now became implacable enemies. The tiger sprang on the buffalo's back to bite her neck, and the buffalo used her horns to pierce the tiger's belly. They rolled on the ground, sprang up again, then rolled again, and fought on and on. Both of them were critically wounded in the deadly struggle.

Meanwhile, the fox had a ringside seat and was enjoying himself laughing and joking. "You two have such super-strength," he laughed. "But compared to my cleverness, you are childish."

Finally the poor tiger flopped down and died. The buffalo too, was bleeding to death. She gave a last kick with her hind legs and as she did, her hoofs struck a sharp rock. The force sent it flying and hit the fox right on his head. Before he could chatter anymore, he dropped down flat on the ground, never to stir again.

# The Buffalo and the Tiger

*A Han Folktale*

In ancient times the buffalo in South China were exceedingly important animals. They labored patiently with the farmer from dawn to dusk in the field as soon as the ground was free of frost and could be broken.

The tiger, on the other hand, was respected but greatly feared. The philosopher, Chuang-tze said, "When you become too intimate with a tiger, measuring his head and arranging his whiskers, how can you avoid the tiger's teeth?"

This folktale however, depicts how the forethought and perseverence of the long-suffering buffalo, not only evades the teeth of the tiger, but proves the merit of labor and loyalty.

A farmer went to the rice field taking his buffalo along to plow. The buffalo sank into the mud and after half a day's work, only a small corner was done. Meanwhile, the farmer cursed and whipped the animal for not being able to pull the plow faster.

"You stupid creature, slow and creeping! You lift your feet only after a lengthy struggle! Haven't you seen a tiger? How fast he runs! How mighty he is! You should learn from the tiger."

The buffalo could hardly stand up from the continuous whipping, and no longer able to bear the cursing, asked impatiently, "What ability does the tiger have? I'm much stronger."

67

The farmer paid no attention to the foolish remarks of the buffalo but just kept on flogging and cursing the beast.

"You belittle me," the buffalo said. "Take me to see the tiger tomorrow. I'll challenge him and let you see with your own eyes, who is the mightier."

The next morning, the farmer took his buffalo to see the tiger. The mighty animal caught the scent of the buffalo and leapt from his lair ready to pounce on his prey. But the buffalo shook his two scythed horns and called out, "Tiger! Tiger! I haven't come to challenge you today, merely to inform you that your teeth are too dull. They won't be able to pierce my heavy skin. Grind them for three days; I'll likewise sharpen my horns. Then we'll fight a duel."

"Readily!" the tiger snarled and disappeared into his den.

The tiger ground his teeth for three days and nights until they were razor sharp. The buffalo also ground his horns, but only for a day. The remaining two days were spent rolling his body in mud and then straw. He repeated the process until his whole body was covered with a heavy layer of clay, black and shiny. Nobody could ever detect the coating of straw.

On the fourth day the tiger and the buffalo met at the appointed spot. The tiger saw the buffalo's body covered with clay and queried, "Why do you cover yourself with clay?"

"To withstand the heat of summer," the buffalo replied. "I roll around the riverbank a few times every day. That's my habit. Everybody knows that."

The tiger eyed the buffalo and thought, "Nothing is wrong with him except that he looks fatter than ever." Then he laughed happily, "Ho! Ho! Ho! Very good! Your flesh looks quite tender. What a tasty meal I'll have!"

"Tiger! Tiger! You may be able to threaten a pig or lamb, but not me. You won't be able to harm me or touch a single hair on my body."

"My teeth were dull three days ago, but even then I'd have dared to eat you," the tiger replied. "Now my teeth are sharp. Do you really think I can't bite you to death?"

"Very well," the buffalo condescended. "Let's see. I'll lie down and let you be the first to bite me three times. If you fail, I'll give you three butts with my horns."

Why would the tiger ever disagree to that? With a dreadful snarl, the powerful tiger pounced on the buffalo, and with mouth wide open, sank his sharp teeth into the buffalo's body. One bite, two, three! Was he dead? Not on your life! Only the cakes of mud filled with straw had fallen apart. As soon as the tiger had finished his third bite, the buffalo got up, lowered his head, and quick as a flash, thrust his curved horns three times into the tiger's body. The first one pierced his stomach, the second, his spine, and the third, hooked his intestines and heart. With that the tiger fell down motionless.

All this time the farmer was watching very closely, and observed how wise and brave the buffalo really was. "Well, that's over," he sighed with relief.

The farmer had been deeply moved, and from that day on cherished his buffalo. There were no more curses, no more "stupid beast" or beatings. Up to now although the buffalo is not very fast at pulling a cart or plowing a field, everyone respects his patience and ability.

# The Diplomat

*A Han Folktale*

This folktale teaches a useful lesson in diplomacy. The characteristics attributed to several animals are well portrayed, depicting the tiger as one to be respected, and if necessary, avoided and the fox as being clever enough to do so.

A tiger, a wolf and a fox who went hunting together, caught a goat, a rabbit and a chicken. Soon after, they sat down to discuss how the spoils should be divided.

The tiger was thinking, "I could eat all three by myself." But he pretended to be fair, and asked the wolf, "How should the spoils be divided? What do you think is fair and square?"

"O, big brother," the wolf replied, "you're the biggest, so you keep the mountain goat. I'll have the rabbit. Let the fox eat the chicken."

The tiger was very dissatisfied and became angry. The wolf was so scared that he ran away lest he become the tiger's next meal.

Turning to the fox, the tiger asked him, "Fox, how would you divide the three?"

"O, King of the forest," the clever fox answered, "you're the biggest, so you could have the chicken for your breakfast, the rabbit for your luncheon, and the goat for your evening meal."

This was what the tiger wanted to begin with, and it pleased him so much that he asked the fox, "Where did you learn to divide with such fair judgment?"

"I learned by observing what happened to the wolf," the fox said. Thereupon he also ran off as fast as he could.

# How Rabbits Got Pink Eyes and Long Ears

*A Chuang Folktale*

The earliest bronze mirrors depicted the rabbit as one of the animals in the zodiac. At varied times in Chinese culture, other animals were used, but the rabbit was never excluded from the twelve. It was regarded as a fertility symbol, classified as Yin, the female, negative principle of the universe. The earliest known story about the rabbit dated back to China's first dynasty, the Hsia, over four thousand years ago, when it became associated with the Autumn Moon Festival. The moon is especially luminous then, and it is said the rabbit may be seen in the moon, standing under a cassia tree. In one paw, the furry creature holds a mortar and in the other a pestle, pounding out the elixir of life. Because of its association with the moon, it acquired the symbolism of immortality and ultimately signified posterity or progeny.

Even today, paper lanterns of fluffy white rabbits having red eyes and long ears are made for the pleasure of young people to celebrate the Autumn Moon Festivities. As soon as evening falls, the lantern is lit by a tiny candle placed within a hollow space of the rabbit's body. Some lanterns have wheels attached so they can be pulled along. If the ground is not quite level, the rabbit will have a realistic bounding movement.

Very dear to the heart of a child and a delight to older people as well, the rabbit lanterns are openly displayed in lantern shops everywhere for the Autumn Moon Festival, one of the most important celebrations of the year.

There was a time when all rabbits had short ears and blue eyes. But that was long ago before one little white rabbit was punished for his greed and impudence. This young rabbit was big and strong—in fact bigger than his mother who took loving care of him. But the bigger he grew, the lazier he became, and the more insolent and arrogant too.

One rainy day while her lazy son stayed inside as usual, the kind old mother rabbit went in search of food. She bounded through the hills, from the meadows to the riverside, but she could not find a thing. A big rain soaked her thoroughly and she was very weary as she returned empty-handed in the dark of night. The spoiled young rabbit was waiting impatiently to snatch whatever his mother brought. He could see that she had nothing and became very angry. "Oh, you're back at last!" he snapped. "Really! I thought you were already dead. Why so late? Do you mean to say you have nothing for me?"

"My child," she answered sadly, "you're no longer a little one. You must not always rely on your mother, but also try to find something to eat yourself."

"Very well then, from now on probably each one is supposed to rely on oneself," he muttered peevishly for he could not stand even this gentle reproach.

The next morning he got up still mumbling, "From now on probably each one is supposed to rely on oneself," and with that took off in a huff. His mother called anxiously to say that she would accompany him. But the offended young rabbit had already disappeared.

"Huh!" he puffed, "Who can't find something to eat, maybe even better than mother." As he ran blindly from place to place, he began to wonder, "Where are all the nice fruits and vegetables?" For all his arrogance, he could not find a thing. "How disappointing! It's a calamity!" he muttered. He soon became tired to death of searching, found a spreading tree and flopped down under its shade to rest. In a twinkling, he was fast asleep.

"Goodness! What was that sound?" he wondered as he awakened with a start. A big wolf was approaching! The rabbit ran as fast as he could. How lucky he had swift legs and could make a dash into a hole that his keen eyes had spotted! The opening was small and the wolf tried scraping at it, but at last gave up. What a narrow escape for the young rabbit! After a while when the frightened rabbit thought the wolf had left, he came out cautiously, and then bounded away in search of something to eat.

At length he came to a pond where water buffalo wallowed. There were many leeches in the pond but, of course, the rabbit did not know about them. He only knew that he was dying of thirst, and without any thought, scampered into the water. A leech promptly fastened itself to the tip of his nose. Oh, such a sudden sharp pain! He had to try very hard, but finally he got rid of the nasty thing. It certainly hurt—and blood oozed from his nose.

As he wandered on tired and hungry, he came upon a beehive. Bzz . . zz . . . the sound attracted him. Alas! How could he know that was not the place to be? Thanks to his swift legs, he managed to escape the angry swarm.

"Wherever could mother have found her tasty food?" he shouted as if challenging something to appear. "Oh well, even she couldn't find anything that rainy day." This time the young rabbit went home empty-handed and hungry in the dark of night. His mother greeted him happily for she had been so worried and was only too glad to see him back safe again.

"Did you manage to find something to eat?" she asked anxiously.

"Of course," he lied.

"You had no trouble, I hope," she said, seeing the blood on his nose.

"No," the rabbit shouted angrily.

His mother could see that he was not telling the truth. But she did not bother him any more.

The following day, he bounded away as it was already

late and he was very hungry. The air was fragrant so he followed the scent that led to fields covered with green. Countless berries grew on bushes, and the fields were filled with vegetables. No one was in sight so he began to nibble on the berries, and even when he had his fill, he ate and ate the fat, juicy turnips that he liked so much. He nibbled a little more on everything and then, almost bursting, took a bundle of turnips and happily went home.

For days, he ate and slept without going to find some food. But when all the turnips were finished, he set out directly for the fields. While he was chewing the tasty turnips, a farmer came along and spied the rabbit. He raised his hoe to strike, but the rabbit dodged. Luckily the blow missed him. But it was close and could have killed him! He bolted from the fields and dashed home again. When his mother saw him trembling, she knew something was wrong. Yet the cheeky little rabbit would not admit it.

The rabbit continued to go to the same fields to steal but always managed to get away on time. "There must be a way to deal with this little thief," the farmer thought to himself. So one day he devised a plan. He boiled a big pot of glutenous rice, put it through a sieve to make a paste, molded it into a human figure, and placed it in his field.

The next day when the rabbit came, he saw the figure watching there. He was scared and did not dare approach. The person did not pay any attention to him so he became bolder, and crept forward slowly and softly. Then he went further and purposely clapped his paws. Still the figure did not move. He became more daring and went in front of the figure, scooped some mud and threw it. There was still no motion. The little rabbit felt safe now and thought, "I can do anything with this fellow." He became so audacious, he called out, "Hello!

Who are you?" There was no answer whereupon he called louder, "Don't you recognize me? I'm the one who often comes to eat your vegetables." There was no sound. The rabbit became angry and shouted, "Why don't you answer me? I won't be polite any longer." Saying that, he raised his right paw and gave the figure a punch. Goodness! His right paw was stuck! But the young rabbit thought the man was holding him so he called in a louder voice, "Hey, let go of me quickly. Ah, still not letting me go—well then, I'll have to give you another punch," he shouted as he thrust out his left paw. Horrors! It also was stuck! "You're not going to let go of me yet, eh! I'm not one to stand ill-treatment." But the rice figure stood silent and motionless.

The rabbit became truly exasperated and shouted, "You deaf and dumb one, still going to hold me! You won't let go of me yet! All right, I'll show you something fiercer." With that, he kicked with his left hind leg and then with his right. Well, well! Now they were both stuck! The rabbit was not only annoyed, he was furious. "Huh, still not letting go of me! I don't believe I can't win a fight with this stupid fellow," he thought to himself. "I'll bump you to death," he cried as he banged his head against the silent figure with all his might. At last the frantic rabbit was firmly stuck and could not budge. He used his whole strength to struggle and his eyes became red and bloodshot.

About that time the farmer came along and laughing aloud, said, "No use to struggle. You can't escape. My sticky rice-man has you glued fast. Now do you dare to steal my vegetables and fruit?"

Only then did the rash young rabbit understand that this man in the field was merely made of paste. He regretted being so arrogant and said, "Uncle farmer, I know that what I did was wrong. I shouldn't steal from you. I want to repent. I'll never again steal from your fields. Please set me free kind uncle."

Since the rabbit recognized his wrong doing, the farmer agreed to let him go. But the rabbit was stuck so firmly—all four paws, his head and whole body, that uncle farmer had to pull very forcefully before the little ears became unstuck. Then he grabbed hold of them, pulling and tugging with all his might. They began to stretch getting longer and longer as he continued to pull all the time the rabbit's eyes grew more pink as he blinked back tears. At last the farmer yanked him loose, looked at the rabbit in dismay and said, "Well, this is your punishment!"

Uncle farmer tried to help the rabbit by wiping all the paste off, but as soon as he was free the happy rabbit bounded away. And that is how rabbits acquired pink eyes and long ears.

# Why Rabbits Live in Burrows

*A Han Folktale*

As discussed in the previous folktale, rabbits have a long history in Chinese culture. These little creatures are beloved by children and enjoyed by adults as well. This is another tale with a happy ending for this favorite animal.

The bear, from ancient to modern times, inhabited the mountains and is notorious for frequenting the country paths, waiting to attack man, woman or child. Of the three animals involved in this folktale, the bear was the first to be associated with history in China's remote past. One of the first battles recorded told of bears who were trained and used in prolonged, bitter warfare.

The wolf also is known to stalk its victims and is considered cunning and sly. Whereas the bear generally symbolized crude power and strength, the wolf represented a heartless schemer. In most tales, as in this one, craftiness and strength were no match for sagacity.

A long time ago, there was a wolf and a grizzly bear who enjoyed eating rabbit. In fact, it was their favorite meat. The forest teemed with rabbits—white ones, mottled and gray. Yet they were never enough for the wolf or bear who relished the little creatures. When the wolf or grizzly approached, the terrified rabbits could only run for it. They often hid under a shrub or among big leaves, their furry tails sticking out. Alas! Such easy prey for the greedy wolf and bear!

One day, quite by chance, a white-haired mother rabbit found a hollow in a tree trunk. She thought this was a good place to hide the small rabbits. But she did not dare let them scamper around to play by themselves, and they became thinner as the days went by.

A gray-haired rabbit came to visit one day, and brought some tender greens.

"Ah, you must have gone afar to find these. Where did you leave your young ones?"

"One of my children is very clever," the visitor replied, "He dug a tunnel in the ground where my whole family can hide. There are three holes connected by tunnels to enter quickly or escape whenever we need."

"Aha," the overjoyed rabbit replied. "What a splendid way for us too!"

It worked so well that all the rabbits seemed to have disappeared. The wolf and bear combed the forest each day but not a trace of a rabbit could be found, and the wolf, who was becoming impatient said, "Perhaps if we hunt together we'll have better luck." But in spite of their efforts they blundered along without success.

One day they happened to find a hole where the rabbits were hiding, and the bear growled, "Let me use my big paw to break the opening, and kill them. At least we'll have one tasty meal."

"Not so quick," the wolf said cautiously. "We had better be more clever and skillful this time. Let's pretend to be friendly and lure the rabbits to play in the forest. Later we can pounce on them. How many rabbits we'll have then!" the wolf leered as he licked his chops in anticipation.

"Very well," the bear agreed. "I'm willing to wait."

Thereupon they went to the entrance of the hideout and tapped in a most friendly way. The mother rabbit peeped through an opening, but beat a hasty retreat.

"Oh, mother rabbit," the cunning wolf called in a beguiling voice, "don't be afraid. We have truly repented. From now on we'll be good friends. You can play anywhere in the forest. We'll never harm you or the wee ones. We'll even protect you against the other animals."

But the white-haired rabbit was no longer foolish or

trusting for she had learned many a sad lesson. She thought to herself, "This will be my chance to get even with them. They are trying to trick me so I'll play a trick on them." She brought out a whistle and a drum, and presenting them to the wolf and the bear said very sweetly, "Since we are now dear friends, I want to give you these gifts. This whistle and drum were treasures handed down from my ancestors. Whenever they are played, all the rabbits come forth from their burrows. Even the mountain goats are attracted and assemble in great numbers. But you must play on the drum loud and clear, and blow the whistle as loud as you can."

The scheming wolf and greedy bear were delirious with joy as they trotted off. The wolf simply could not wait any longer, so after walking a short distance, he began to blow on the whistle to see how it would work—*toot, toot.* No sooner had the first sound pierced the air when a hunter concealed somewhere in the forest, aimed his rifle. B A N G! Down went the wolf without a howl.

Meanwhile the bear remembered there was a plump goat in a farmer's yard so he raced on far ahead of the wolf. He beat on the drum for all he was worth—*boom, boom.* The farmer within his hut was alerted by the sound, and peering through the crack, saw the bear approaching. Taking up his rifle, he aimed carefully. B A N G! Down tumbled the bear, and lay motionless!

For quite some time the rabbits found peace in the forest, and could go wherever they wished to seek the greens they liked so much. But to this day they make their homes under the earth with three holes connected by long tunnels in case they have to escape.

# The Popeyed Dragonfly and the Earthworm

*A Han Folktale*

All over China, there are many dragonflies and they flit about in droves. Children are fascinated by their movement and catch them to play with like pets. The character writing for the word dragonfly is one of the first to be taught a young child. Artists are also endeared to the dragonfly which was a popular subject for painting during a number of dynasties. Sung artists especially, captured the ethereal beauty of this lovely insect, poised or in flight.

In ancient times, the earthworm had a pair of very good eyes. But then one day while baking herself in the sun, she overheard a dragonfly complaining about her eyesight, mutter, "I can fly swiftly. If only I had better eyes to see farther."

The kindhearted worm instantly beckoned the dragonfly and said, "I have a pair of good eyes that I can lend you. But please remember to return them as soon as you can."

The dragonfly assured the earthworm she would indeed return them and thanked her for the kindness. On receiving them, she placed them above her own, and to her great surprise and delight, found that she now had a double pair of eyes. They bulged a little, but she could see far into the distance. She was ever so gleeful as she flew over the land.

By sunset, the bighearted worm began to feel uneasy. She waited long past twilight, but the dragonfly did not appear. What should she do? The terrified worm crawled under the earth for the night. The next morning she crept out and from time to time called in a pleading voice, "Dragonfly! Dragonfly! Please remember I need my eyes. Please remember." But the dragonfly was nowhere in sight.

Meanwhile, the happy dragonfly flitted past hills, winding streams and pathways without end. Weaving in and out of foliage and flower scented gardens, she reached a pond filled with lotus. Amid the tall, elegant grass, she caught sight of a frog taking care of her little ones. They were so lively jumping on the lotus leaves,

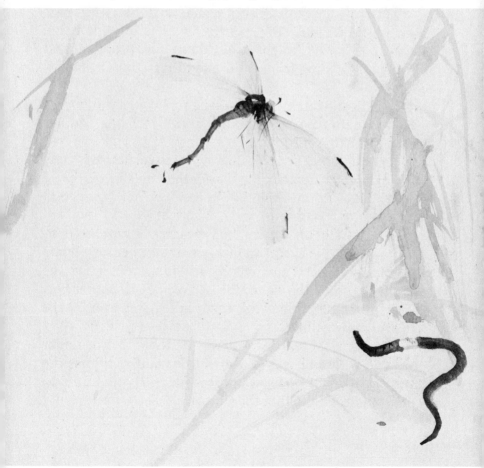

leaping onto rocks and over one another. "Cr-oak, cr-oak, cr-oak . . . ." They seemed to be saying, "What fun! What fun! Oh such fun!"

"Ah," the dragonfly sighed, "I'd like to raise my little ones in a pond. Will you show me how?" she begged the frog.

The frog was only too happy to help. But as the days passed, the dragonfly found that when her young ones changed their forms several times, naughty children often snatched them from the water and destroyed them. It was really very sad!

"This will never do," she began to think. "My own way was after all, the better one." Thereupon she decided to speak to the frog about the problem and simply said, "Frog friend, I'd like to raise my little ones as before."

"But it's too late now," the frog replied very annoyed. "How can you possibly change now? Perhaps Mother Earth can help you."

The dragonfly hurriedly flew away to seek advice. Only then did she remember the worm and went in search of her. She flew far and wide, high and low, calling as loud as she could, "Where are you? Where are you?"

By this time, the worm had become accustomed to staying under the earth. In fact, she found her new home cool in summer and comfortable in winter. Whenever she left the bosom of the earth, the sun seemed to bother her. So she remained under the earth and never even heard the dragonfly calling.

Thereafter the earthworm was content to live under the earth without her eyes. But the dragonfly still has the borrowed pair of popeyes and continues to circle round and round trying to find the worm.

# Three Blind Men and an Elephant

*A Han Folktale*

Although this folktale is classified as being of Chinese derivation, India has a similar one, and so does Africa. However, the philosophical note is typically Chinese even though the basic thought is universal: When a person is opinionated or blind to his limitations because of insufficient knowledge or smug mentality, he is as blind as if he had no eyesight.

One day, three blind men happened to meet each other and gossiped a long time about many things. Suddenly one of them recalled, "I heard that an elephant is a queer animal. Too bad we're blind and can't see it."

"Ah, yes, truly too bad we don't have the good fortune to see the strange animal," another one sighed.

The third one, quite annoyed, joined in and said, "See? Forget it! Just to feel it would be great."

"Well, that's true. If only there were some way of touching the elephant, we'd be able to know," they all agreed.

It so happened that a merchant with a herd of elephants was passing, and overheard their conversation. "You fellows, do you really want to feel an elephant? Then follow me; I will show you," he said.

The three men were surprised and happy. Taking one another's hand, they quickly formed a line and followed while the merchant led the way. Each one began to contemplate how he would feel the animal, and tried to figure how he would form an image.

After reaching their destination, the merchant asked them to sit on the ground to wait. In a few minutes he led the first blind man to feel the elephant. With outstretched hand, he touched first the left foreleg and then the right. After that he felt the two legs from the top to the bottom, and with a beaming face, turned to say, "So, the queer animal is just like that." Then he slowly returned to the group.

Thereupon the second blind man was led to the rear of the elephant. He touched the tail which wagged a few times, and he exclaimed with satisfaction, "Ha! Truly a queer animal! Truly odd! I know now. I know." He hurriedly stepped aside.

The third blind man's turn came, and he touched the elephant's trunk which moved back and forth turning and twisting and he thought, "That's it! I've learned."

The three blind men thanked the merchant and went their way. Each one was secretly excited over the experience and had a lot to say, yet all walked rapidly without saying a word.

"Let's sit down and have a discussion about this queer animal," the second blind man said, breaking the silence.

"A very good idea. Very good," the other two agreed for they also had this in mind.

Without waiting for anyone to be properly seated, the second one blurted out, "This queer animal is like our straw fans swinging back and forth to give us a breeze. However, it's not so big or well made. The main portion is rather wispy."

"No, no!" the first blind man shouted in disagreement. "This queer animal resembles two big trees without any branches."

"You're both wrong," the third man replied. "This queer animal is similar to a snake; it's long and round, and very strong."

How they argued! Each one insisted that he alone was correct. Of course, there was no conclusion for not one had thoroughly examined the whole elephant. How can anyone describe the whole until he has learned the total of the parts?

# Fifteen Honest Coins

*A Han Folktale*

This is one of the many tales about a magistrate named Pao Kung who lived during the Sung Dynasty. The law was carried out by him whether a suspect was a high official or merely a peasant. He was incorruptible, and refused to compromise his worthy principles. There was a saying at the capital, "If you can't straighten your grievances, go to old Pao who is like the god of the nether world." After his death, he was worshipped as the Demon God who presided over the nether world and punished all who committed crimes.

Although Pao Kung was esteemed by the common people and honest scholars, he was greatly feared by corrupt officials. He was a serious person who rarely smiled. According to a saying, "If ever Pao Kung smiled, the (muddy) Yellow River would be clean."

In a little village remote from the hustle and bustle of the city, there once lived a poor old woman and her son. Every day they arose before dawn to gather twigs from the nearby mountains. When the sun arose, he was already carrying the bundles to the marketplace while his mother returned to their thatched hut to attend the household chores. With the money from the firewood, he usually bought some oil, rice, vegetables and occasionally, a few eggs or a very small amount of meat. By noon, he would be on his way home. Without exception this was their daily, simple way of life.

One morning when he went to the marketplace there was the usual crowd bargaining, but nobody came to purchase his twigs. As he waited patiently he suddenly caught sight of a small bag lying near his twigs. "Someone must have dropped it," he mused, and looking hastily into the bag, saw some coins. Without waiting any longer, he hurried home.

"Why have you come back so early today?" his mother queried.

"I had good luck! I found this bag containing some coins. The firewood wasn't sold, but perhaps whatever is in the bag will make up for it," he replied.

The mother and son eagerly opened the bag to count the coins that amounted to fifteen in all.

"Someone must be very unhappy over the loss," she sighed. "My son, you must return this to the owner. He may need it—just like us—to buy rice and oil. His family may even be starving," she added trying to persuade him to hurry.

"But Ma-ma, I've never seen the owner. To whom should I give the money?"

"Just stay at the same spot where you found the money and wait until someone comes looking for it. I won't feel comfortable keeping these coins. I insist that you go right now."

So he returned to the marketplace and stood there to watch the passing crowds. It was approaching noon and the morning market was almost over when a merchant walked by. He turned his head in all directions as if searching for something.

"Good master! What are you looking for? Have you lost something?"

"Yes, I'm looking for a purse. I must have dropped it somewhere in the marketplace."

"Well then, is this yours?" the young fellow asked extending the bag.

"It certainly is!" the merchant exclaimed as he snatched it and began counting the coins: "One, two, three, four, five . . . fifteen! Why—how is that—only fifteen! I had thirty coins in my purse," he shouted angrily. "You must have kept fifteen for yourself. How dare you return my purse with only half the money!"

"There were only fifteen coins. I'm an honest person. Really I am, truly, truly," the youth pleaded.

An argument started, and in no time at all a big crowd gathered to hear what was happening. The argument went on endlessly, each accusing the other of dishonesty. At last the crowd urged them to see Pao Kung, the magistrate. The whole procession followed them to the *yamen* where the two angry fellows were given a hearing.

"How many coins did you find in that bag?" the magistrate asked the youth.

"Fifteen."

"Did you count the coins by yourself?" the magistrate inquired.

"No, my mother and I opened the bag and we counted them together."

Thereupon the magistrate asked a petty officer to fetch the mother instantly.

"How many coins did you count in the bag?" the magistrate questioned her.

"There were fifteen coins. I urged my son to go back to the same spot in the marketplace where he picked up the bag, and wait for the owner so it could be returned."

The magistrate looked at the old woman and the youth from head to foot. After this appraisal, he asked the merchant, "How much money have you lost?"

"I lost thirty coins. That fellow returned only fifteen. He has kept fifteen. He is dishonest. I want my thirty coins," he yelled in a demanding voice.

The magistrate looked at the merchant from head to foot, and after this scrutiny, a faint smile passed over his face. Then suddenly banging on the table for attention so that all could hear, he turned to the merchant and said, "Since you maintain that you have lost a purse with thirty coins, this bag with only fifteen, is clearly not yours. Therefore you cannot claim it."

Then addressing the youth, the magistrate continued, "Since you found this bag containing fifteen coins and no one has claimed rightful ownership, you may keep it to purchase some food for your old mother. The case is now closed."

Everyone in the courtroom felt satisfied with the wise, just decision of the magistrate.

# The Smell of Food and Jingle of Coins

*A Kazakh Folktale*

In the past when a man was very poor, even though he spoke a hundred tongues, who would ever listen to him or lend a helping hand? Hogranasr! the popular hero and champion of the poor and oppressed. He lived among the Kazakh in the north and northwest regions of Sinkiang Province which border the United Soviet Socialist Republics.

In a certain village one day, a restaurant proprietor was beating a customer. He kept on striking and pounding the fellow until even his ragged dress was badly torn. The dreadful commotion attracted a large number of onlookers. Hogranasr was passing by, and being just as curious, pushed his way through the crowd. Then stepping forward, he separated the two men.

"Why are you beating him?" he asked the fat proprietor.

"This penniless beggar tried to slip out without paying me," the proprietor replied indignantly.

"What did he eat and how much does he owe you?"

"He occupied a table in my restaurant, pulled out a bun, and sat there a long time without ordering anything. When his bun was flavored with the fragrance from my kitchen, he ate it. He has to pay for that. Who can get the smell of food for nothing?"

"What you say sounds reasonable," Hogranasr replied. "Now then what do you have to say?" he asked turning to the poor man.

"Yes, I went to his restaurant and sat at a table, but the food cost too much so I ate my own bun. Do you think I should pay for that?"

"What you say is also reasonable," Hogranasr said thoughtfully. "But tell me, do you have any money at all?"

"Only a few coins."

"Then give them to me, and get along with you," the fat proprietor said, eagerly stretching out his hand.

"Please be patient, proprietor. Please stay away for a while," Hogranasr pleaded. "Let me get the money out of his pocket first." He then whispered a few words into the poor man's ear, took the coins from him, and beckoned the proprietor to come near. Cupping his hands, Hogranasr shook the coins and asked the proprietor, "Do you hear the sound?"

"Yes, thank you very much," he nodded, thinking that they were being given to him and ready to grasp them.

Hogranasr then returned the coins to the pauper.

"What are you doing?" the bewildered proprietor shouted.

"Well, I just want to be fair," Hogranasr replied dispassionately. "He only smelled your fragrant food, but didn't eat any. Now you have heard the jingle of his coins but didn't get them. You both got a satisfactory bargain. The smell of your food is worth no more than the jingle of his coins. What more do you expect?"

# The Stone Mason

*A T'ung Folktale*

The hard-working T'ung people inhabit the border regions of Kweichow, Hunan and Kwangsi Provinces. The people are noted for their fine singing, and splendid embroidery, practically every woman being an expert.

This T'ung folktale skillfully portrays some aspects of their past life as seen through the eyes of a Han who lived among the T'ung people. The gap between the wealthy class and the common folk was too great. Even the Han had many grievances, and of course this was especially true of the minorities who did not have a good relationship with the Han officials.

In ancient times there was a stone mason who lived nearby the T'ung tribe. He was a good craftsman and was well-known for his dexterity. One day he was asked by a wealthy merchant to chisel a stone grinder. At the sight of the mansion he could only stand there gaping. "Ah! Such a big, grand house! What splendor and magnificence!" When he saw the people dressed in fine silk and satin leisurely being served rare and precious food, he marveled at the elegance and comfort. "If only I could be a rich man!" he exclaimed. Day after day he dreamed about it and soon completely ceased working.

A fairy in heaven heard his wish and granted it. The stone mason was then exceedingly happy.

After some time a high official passed through his village. Surrounding the sedan chair that carried him were foot soldiers calling out to the populace to make way. They beat drums and struck gongs, and everyone scattered. Everyone bowed low as the sedan chair went by. "How powerful that official must be!" the stone mason thought to himself, when they approached his house. "This official has foot soldiers following him on the right side, the left, in front and back. But I also have attendants. Why should I pay homage to him?" So he did not bow low.

"Bind that fellow," the high official ordered. "Give him three hundred lashes and fine him three hundred pieces of silver. That will teach him a lesson in respect!"

After the official left the stone mason got up from the ground and sighed, "Ah yo! An official is even more powerful than a rich merchant." From that time on he wished only to be a high official.

When the fairy heard his wish, she readily granted it. Once again the stone mason was truly happy.

The stone mason then assumed all the airs of a high official, imitated all their wrong-doings, and was hated by everyone. One day his sedan chair passed a hillside where a group of young, lovely T'ung maidens were gathering firewood. His troop pounced on them like hungry tigers after a flock of sheep. Their shouts and call for help could be heard far away. All of a sudden there was a great commotion, and the entire hillside was covered with T'ung tribesmen each carrying a knife, ax, plow or spear. They rushed over screaming, "Strike! Kill!" They bound the troop together and shoved them along to the T'ung village where they were given a sound thrashing. After that they were set free.

From that time on the stone mason did not dare to imitate a high official but he kept thinking, "I figured the high official was almighty. Compared to the T'ung people, he is insignificant!" He now swore that he only wished to be one of the T'ung tribesmen.

Again the fairy heard his wish and granted it. This time he was so happy that he laughed with his eyes half-closed and his mouth wide-open. He could hardly manage to open his eyes or close his mouth again.

Now that the stone mason had become a T'ung tribesman he worked as they did from morning to night without stop in the fields or on the hillsides. That summer the sun shone like a ball of fire scorching his skin and almost making him faint. Even the birds and animals hid in the shade of the deep forest, and buffalo wallowed in the cool, muddy water. Only the tender green rice sprouts seemed brave enough to lift their heads like the stubborn T'ung people capable of suffering and withstanding ordeals. "Ah, the sun is the fiercest, the most powerful of all!" he cried out and with that began to dream of being the sun.

The fairy granted him his wish and placed him high in the sky so that his burning rays could shine everywhere, and people would be afraid of his presence.

One day a black cloud suddenly came from the west and swept over the sky covering the sun like a blanket. "Hey!" he shouted, "It's fierce to be the sun, but who knew that a black cloud was so much mightier!"

So now he wished to be a cloud, and the fairy having granted his wish, let him float around freely in the sky.

But one day without any warning a sudden gust of wind came along and blew him apart. "Ah yo! How strong the wind is blowing!" he cried out. "I'm being torn to pieces! I have no place to hide! I don't want to be a black cloud anymore. I want to become the wind!"

Thereupon the fairy granted his wish.

With that, he used all his might to blow, breaking houses and uprooting trees. How fierce he was!

One day as he tore over the land, he blew against a boulder. But it did not budge, and then the stone mason thought, "My breath can blow everything down except a boulder. If I could become a boulder that would be the best of all!"

His wish was instantly granted, and the fairy placed him on the top of a high mountain. No one dared to touch him there.

Time passed until one day, a group of stone masons came along. They climbed to the mountaintop, looked all around the boulder very carefully and nodded their heads. "Yes, that's the one," they said, and without another word, began to chisel and cut him to pieces. The stone mason was terrified, and begged the fairy for help.

"Isn't it still best to be a mason?" the fairy asked in reply, and immediately transformed him into one of the stone masons.

From then on he did not indulge in idle dreams, but worked diligently at all times chiseling stone-grinders. He worked better and faster than ever before, and became known for his craftsmanship. All the T'ung tribespeople respected him as a stone mason.

# The Jealous Artist and the Architect

*A Mongolian Folktale*

The Mongols were nomads with no cultural heritage or continuity in their history. When such leaders as Jenghis Khan or Kubilai Khan were strong and ambitious, their armies swept over many lands like a whirlwind over a desert. Yet only three decades after these men passed away, the Yuan kingdoms disintegrated and the Mongols retreated to the steppe where they resumed their former ordinary nomadic life. It was as though a mirage had appeared and then simply faded.

According to a Yuan Dynasty recording, when Jenghiz Khan was dying, he called his four heirs to his bedside. Giving them four bundles of arrows, he told each man to break a bundle. Since they were unable, he had them try to break the arrows singly. This was done easily, whereupon he gave them counsel and said, "Unity is strength."

Although the Khan divided his vast domains among his heirs, the Mongol chieftains chose Ogodai, his third son to be the Grand Khan of the entire domains. Struggle for power, jealousy and revenge with ruthless killing of brothers and relatives, dominated Mongol sovereignty, and weakened a once vigorous people. These factors, and superstition, responsible for some of the slaughter, contributed to the eventual downfall of the dynasty.

There was once an old Khan who ruled over the tribes in Mongolia. Since he had no brothers sovereignty was passed to his only son after he died. Two gifted men, one an artist, the other an architect, served him faithfully. But they were not compatible and often quarreled because of jealousy.

96

One day the artist decided that he could not tolerate the architect any longer and contrived a way to get rid of him. He prepared a piece of sheepskin, making it appear very old with strange decorations and mystic writing, and presenting it to the Khan said, "This piece of parchment fell from heaven."

The Khan examined it, but unable to make anything of the writing, asked, "Can you read what it says?"

The artist studied it, and at length said, "This is a letter sent by your deceased father. Briefly, it says that he has been fortunate and is quite happy in heaven. He is asking you to send a good architect immediately to build a palace for him as nobody there knows how. The method of sending the architect is clearly stated. A large pile of wood is all that is required. The architect will then be able to rise with the smoke. After the building is completed, he will be sent down to earth again."

The architect was summoned and told about the message from the old Khan. "This is the trickery of the artist," he instantly thought. Yet he said, "Very well. I only ask Your Highness to grant me a week to settle my household affairs."

This being granted, the architect returned to his family and immediately had his servants dig a tunnel from his house to the corner of the open square where the grains were threshed and public functions took place. Afterward, he ordered them to loosen one of the large stone slabs. They labored day and night, and after a week had passed, the architect appeared before the Khan. Instructions were given for firewood to be placed on the corner of the square above the slabs. The architect sat on the firewood while more was piled around him until it almost covered him. The Khan and officials stood around to watch. Thick black smoke began to roll out and rapidly enveloped the architect. At that moment he fell down feigning death. In reality, he rapidly and skillfully removed the wood under him, lifted the slab, and crept into the tunnel thereby escaping to a secret room in his house.

His relatives and family members wept to show their grief; the spectators admired his fortitude. They believed that he had ascended to heaven since there was no trace of charred remains. Meanwhile, the architect stayed in the secret room for a month. Taking only light food and a small quantity of goat's milk, he became quite thin, and the dark, sunless room gave his skin a deathlike pallor. He had his wife buy a suit of white silk, and a few lengths of fine silk, that he had made into a turban. In this odd costume, making him look like an apparition, he went to see the Khan.

"You have actually returned!" the Khan exclaimed. "Have you finished the building? How is my father? Are there any instructions from him?"

The architect nodded and silently presented a letter that read, "My dear son — Thank you for your architect's help. The palace is now completed, but the walls, ceiling and beams need decorations. There is no gifted artist here so I am asking you to send someone. Use the method as before."

The artist was thereupon summoned. He was greatly surprised to see the pale, unearthly looking architect, and figured that he had really gone to heaven and returned. And with this comforting thought, he said in a grandiose manner, "Of course, I'll be willing."

The same ceremony was performed for the artist as he himself had plotted for the architect, only this time there was no loosened stone.

# How the Moon and Stars Were Created

*A Yao Folktale*

There were other versions of this folktale throughout China that were essentially oral in tradition and all had one thing in common—superstition. Although reflecting early man's beliefs, in a sense they also recorded the troublous beginnings of the world. The calamities that beset mankind and the phenomena that were observed but could not be explained, formed the basis of these tales. Earthquakes, volcanic eruptions, floods, draught or avalanche brought suffering and created fears. Eclipse of the sun or moon, appearance of a rainbow, thunder, lightning or a shooting star caused wonder and much apprehension. Many ancient folktales revolved around such happenings.

The Yao people dwell in Kwangsi Province, the northern part of Kwangtung, and the southwestern and western part of Hunan near the Kweichow border. These regions have spectacular mountains, some appearing like a forest of pinnacles and spires. People who have never visited there regard the fantastic forms depicted by Chinese traditional painters, as imaginary whereas they are in reality a genuine presentation of the landscape. It must have taken millenniums before the mountainous, odd shapes evolved and many dire happenings must have taken place.

The Yao men were intrepid hunters, famed for their skill with the bow and arrow; the women were noted for their splendid embroidery and weaving.

In extreme antiquity, there were no moon or stars. Only the sun shone in the sky, and after the sun had set and night fell, the heavens were entirely black.

Then one night an intensely hot moon suddenly appeared. It was not square or round, but had seven pinnacles and eight corners, and was like a volcanic rock emitting poisonous rays with innumerable fiery arrows. All the tender leaves of the crops were scorched, and mankind suffered from the heat far into the night.

"Ah, Heaven! We don't want this fiery moon," the men and womenfolk cried aloud, unable to sleep or breathe. "We are nearly perishing from this poisonous, oppressive heat," they complained as sweat rolled down their cheeks.

At that time, there was a young couple living at the foot of a big, stone mountain. The man, named Ya Lah, was an expert archer who did nothing but climb mountains and hunt. The woman, named Ni Ngau, was a skillful weaver who worked at her loom the livelong day. "This fiery moon is unbearable," she said to her husband one day. "It has brought so much hardship to people. You are a clever archer—why not shoot down the moon and save mankind?"

Ya Lah patted his chest, took up his bow and arrow, and bravely climbed to the mountaintop. He clenched his teeth, gathered all his strength to draw the bow to the fullest, and shot an arrow straight toward the moon. The arrow zipped through the sky halfway to the moon and then fell to earth. He continued shooting one hundred times, but all fell to earth after reaching only halfway. Alas! There were no more arrows. Looking upward he saw the fiery moon still overhead; looking downward to the foot of the mountains, he saw the scorched, tender leaves of the crops, and the starved, hollow-cheeked faces of the people. Ya Lah sighed helplessly.

All of a sudden, he heard *yi-ya,* something creak behind him. A big rock opened like a door, and an old man with a long white beard, emerged. "In the Southern Mountain," he said, "there dwells the tiger; in the Northern Mountain, there, the tall deer. You must eat the flesh of the tiger to gain great strength. The tiger's tail make into a bow; the tiger's tendon use for a bowstring; the deer's horn, for your arrow. Then shoot the moon till it spins, spins, spins."

Having spoken, he disappeared into the rock. The stone door again creaked, 'yi-ya,' and closed behind him.

It was clear to Ya Lah what the old man was telling him; so he quickly climbed down the mountainside and returned to discuss with his wife the way to catch the tiger and the deer.

"You are an expert archer," his wife reminded him. "Just shoot them with your bow and arrow."

"I've already tried. My arrows can't pierce the thick, tough hides of the Southern Mountain tiger or the Northern Mountain deer. The only way is to use a net to trap them. But where can I find a net stout and large enough?"

Ni Ngau thought for a while and then felt her own hair. "Use my hair to make a net," she said as she pulled out her hairs which somehow instantly grew back again and again like a magic silkworm spinning threads to make a cocoon.

Thirty days and nights were spent weaving a net complete with a fastener. The archer and his wife then journeyed to the Southern Mountain where they set the net in front of a tiger's den. Not long after a tiger was trapped within the net. The beast struggled, rolled in anger, and growled with all his might, shaking the mountain valleys. But the young couple bravely killed the tiger and brought it home. Then they journeyed to the Northern Mountain, trapped and killed a deer in the same way, and brought the tall deer home.

Ya Lah ate the flesh of the big tiger, and his strength increased ten thousandfold. He made a bow and bowstring with the tiger's tail and tendon, and an arrow with the deer's horn, and then climbed to the top of the stone mountain once more. Drawing his mighty bow to the fullest, with all his strength he let fly the arrow. This time the arrow whistled straight to the moon. With a thunderous roar, sparks of fire shot forth from the moon, scattered and became stars. The arrow bounded back to Ya Lah who continued to shoot it a hundred times. All the irregular corners of the moon were chipped off and the whole sky was filled with stars. The moon was then sent spinning. However, the heat had not diminished, and the poisonous rays still scorched the young leaves, and made people miserable. Ya Lah climbed down the mountainside very disheartened.

"Ni Ngau, what should we do?" he asked her. "The moon is still ejecting hot, poisonous rays! If only we had something to cover the moon."

At the time that Ya Lah spoke, Ni Ngau was busy weaving a very lovely brocade. The pattern was white sheep and rabbits in a meadow beyond a house. At the entrance was a cassia tree with tiny golden, fragrant flowers, and Ni Ngau's image sitting under the tree. She was just about to weave her husband's image when she heard his wish, and so she said, "Please take this beautiful brocade, tie it to your arrowhead and shoot it to cover the heat of the moon."

Ya Lah went to the mountaintop to do as his wife suggested, and the moon was completely covered. The hot, poisonous rays ceased to pour forth, and the moon became pale and white, cool and lovable instead. The people at the foot of the mountain, laughed and danced with joy at the sight.

The archer remained on the mountaintop admiring the new moon when suddenly he saw his wife's image, the white sheep and rabbits beginning to move. The image was beckoning, and Ni Ngau, who was standing in front of her own door admiring the moon, began to float like a feather toward the sky. When she reached the moon, she mingled with her image and became one.

As Ya Lah gazed at this strange happening, he became so frustrated that his legs began to wobble. Sitting down on a rock, he stared wide-eyed at the moon, and shouted with long wailing cries, "Ni Ngau! Ah, why didn't you weave me in the brocade? Oh my Ni Ngau, please come down. Ni Ngau! Please come down."

Ni Ngau was likewise excited, her heart jumping fast. She tugged at her hair until it stretched and then plaited it into a braid. When the moon spun in the heavens and reached above the mountaintop, she dipped her head and let her queue drop to the mountaintop. Ya Lah caught hold of it, and climbed like a monkey all the way up to the moon. They both held tightly to each other's hand. How happy they were to be together again!

So when you see the faint shadows in the moon, they are Ya Lah and Ni Ngau. She is sitting under the fragrant cassia tree busy with her weaving. Ya Lah is herding the white sheep and white rabbits.

# General Ma Yuan's Arrow

*A Han Folktale*

There is a pass at the southern extremity of Kwangsi Province. Even today you can observe holes through three mountains in Kweiliu, Yansao and Chen Nan. Chen Nan Kwan was the garrison pass between ancient China and the boundary of the southern tribe's territory. *Chen Nan* which meant "Conquer the South"; however, the name was recently changed to *Yu I* meaning "Friendship" or "Goodwill Pass." It is near the border of what is now North Vietnam.

This folktale describes how the holes in the mountains came to be. General Ma Yuan was a brave, powerful chieftain of the Tatar tribes. He was defeated in battle with the Han whose victorious general treated him with equality and won him over to serve the Han Dynasty. He died during one of his campaigns, fighting to the end of his life for the Han sovereign. He was an outstanding example of the Confucian ideal of serving the ruler and country, faithfully.

During the Han Dynasty there was a rebellion of the *Nan Man* (southern barbarians) in Kwangsi Province. The emperor sent large armies to subdue the tribes but it was a dismal failure. He became so worried that he ordered all of his generals and premiers to a conference over which he personally presided.

Some officials advised the emperor to dispatch large armies by many different routes to encircle the rebels. Others suggested uniting two neighboring kingdoms for a concerted attack. A certain number advocated sending a beautiful princess as a wife for the barbarian chieftain, the union thereby eliminating the need to conquer them. But the emperor was not satisfied with any of the suggestions.

Finally Ma Yuan, the Tatar general stood up to say, "Your Highness, don't worry about this rebellion. Just allow me to go with a platoon of soldiers. I can guarantee that I will subdue the *Nan Man.*"

A faint smile passed over the emperor's face as he replied, "General Ma, you have served the country loyally enough. I shall not trouble you this time."

Hearing his sovereign's remark, Ma Yuan realized that the emperor thought he was far too old for active warfare, and was very downcast. Returning home, he gathered several dozens of his own trusted, elderly soldiers and bodyguards, and set out for Kwangsi Province without letting the emperor know.

When they reached Kweilin, they camped on the bank of the Li River. The sentinel of the southern tribes saw them and immediately blew his horn as a warning. In a short time a swarm of soldiers covered the mountainside and plains. Ma Yuan's soldiers were inwardly uneasy when they saw such large numbers of enemy soldiers. But General Ma rode his horse back and forth along the riverbank with the utmost composure.

After a while a long horn sounded another signal across the river. The tribes instantly spread out in single line formation. Behind them came a large banner and a burly general riding a big horse. This was their chieftain. He rode straight to the front where he recognized old General Ma on the opposite side of the river, and laughing aloud, said, "Ma Yuan, Ma Yuan, you ancient one, still alive! Why don't you go back to enjoy your old age? What do you want to come here for? Your little platoon isn't enough for my horse's hooves to trample on."

Ma Yuan slowly ran his fingers through his beard and calmly replied, "Don't be so boastful. Though I am old, my skill in archery has not grown rusty." Pulling out an arrow and pointing at a rock on the other side of the mountain, he said, "Have a look. See that rock on the mountain there. Now watch my arrow."

There was a sound of who-oo-ooo . . . .' Everybody heard the whir of the arrow flying across the river and almost simultaneously an explosive sound—'wha-la'! And that big stone on the mountainside had disappeared! There was a huge hole right through the mountain, and the sky on the other side was now visible.

Lowering his bow, Ma Yuan called to the chieftain, "Let me ask you—is your chest harder than the rock of that mountain?"

The chieftain and his soldiers were dumbfounded. Whatever courage they had before was lost after seeing his prowess. But only after hearing what Ma Yuan said, did they really seem to wake up, and then they fled with all possible speed.

However, this strange arrow—after piercing the mountain continued circling in the sky with the same big sound, 'who-oo-ooo . . . .' chasing after the chieftain and his soldiers all the way to the district of Yangsao where there was yet another mountain, and again a bang—'wha-la', and a hole pierced that mountain. The men fled further and further but the arrow chased them until they reached Chen Nan Kwan where there was yet another mountain. Only then did the arrow drop to the ground.

The Southern Barbarian chieftain had retreated all the way beyond the southern border of the garrison pass and thereafter never again dared to cross into Han territory. Thus General Ma Yuan's one arrow successfully quashed the rebellious tribes and the mountains still bear the mark of his bloodless victory.

# How the Sea Became Salty

*A Han Folktale*

As far back into the past as one can delve, salt was considered a precious commodity, and eagerly sought by mankind.

Han Wu Ti, an emperor of the Han Dynasty, took over the collection of revenue from salt to help his depleted treasury. Thereafter, salt was monopolized by the government in power. Salt wells provided a big source of income, especially those in what is now Szechwan, one of the richest provinces in China. Special officers were stationed there to supervise the salt production and collect revenue. Many wars were fought to gain control of this province.

How valuable salt was to man may be judged from this ancient folktale of the greedy official who coveted salt that could give him untold riches, even though he already had position and wealth.

A long time ago there were two brothers such as I'll tell you about. The younger one, Ti Ti, stayed at home with his mother to work in the fields. The elder brother, Ko Ko, went away to become an official. Months and years passed, but not once did he return to pay them a visit.

One year during a draught, the mother thought of her elder son on his birthday, and told the younger one, "Go to Ko Ko's official residence and ask him to visit us during his spare time."

But Ti Ti was unwilling to go and said, "Mother, he's an official. He has forgotten us long ago. Even if I go, he won't pay any attention to me."

"Just go! Say that mother asked you. Won't he even remember his mother? You might bring back some food that we need so badly. Such difficult times!" she sighed.

So the young son obeyed and set out for the city. When

he reached the elder brother's residence he observed much activity and excitement. Guests wearing splendid robes of red and green were arriving to celebrate the master's birthday. The best cooks available in the city had been summoned for the occasion. The big kitchen was filled with servants busily preparing for the banquet.

Ti Ti went straight in. No one stopped him since he looked like one of the attendants. He went from one courtyard to another, looking around until he reached a great hall and spotted his elder brother exchanging greetings with the official visitors. Approaching noiseless he timidly called, "Ko Ko."

It seemed that Ko Ko did not recognize him. But after relaying the message from his mother, the official quickly pretended to be concerned, and said, "You came just on time. I've longed to see you and mother." After these brief words he ordered his servant to lead Ti Ti away.

Before long the banquet began with hundreds of people taking seats at varied tables. Steaming hot fish, chicken and innumerable dishes, the names unknown to him, passed in front of his eyes, to be spread on the tables. Amidst the movement of servants to and fro, came the sound of merriment. People drank wine and played a guessing game as they thrust out their fingers, calling, "One and three and . . . " to see who would win or lose. If the number called matched the fingers thrust out, the caller was the winner and the loser drank the wine bottoms up.

Ti Ti was brought into the kitchen to eat with the helpers. Later, one of the cooks wrapped a big meat bone in a lotus leaf, slipped it without any fuss into Ti Ti's hand, and whispered, "It's enough for a meal. Better take it back with you." Remembering how anxiously his old mother must be waiting, he carefully placed it next to his bosom and hastily left without saying good-bye to Ko Ko.

It was getting late when Ti Ti finally got out of the city; so he quickened his pace, intent only on reaching home as early as possible. Suddenly he heard a voice from the roadside say, "How delicious! Young fellow, what good things are you carrying?"

Ti Ti turned to look. The voice came from an old woman digging wild greens nearby. "Yes, old Ma-ma," he replied.

"What are they? Smells like something good to eat."

"Only a big meat bone."

"Oh! I'm so hungry! Will you give me some?"

"Old Ma-ma, I'm bringing this for my mother."

"Just a small piece of meat," the old woman implored. "I'm so hungry!"

Ti Ti deliberated for a while, slowly took the bone from his bosom, tore a piece of meat from it and gave it to the old woman.

"Truly delicious, young fellow," she said after finishing. "I'll tell you—not far from here is a mountain cave where seven maidens dwell. They are almost starving. You should go there to share some meat with them also."

"How can I do that? This is for my mother."

"Young fellow, they won't eat and then forget you. Better go. Otherwise before you know, they will have starved to death."

The softhearted Ti Ti followed the direction where the old woman pointed. Truly, there was the mountain cave with the seven maidens within exactly as the old woman had said. He approached them without saying a word, slowly took the meat bone from his bosom, placed it on a stone table and turned to leave. A voice behind him called out, "Brother! Stop!" the eldest maiden came forward and said, "You truly have a good heart. Do you want anything? There are so many things here. Take whatever you wish."

For the first time he observed the jade articles, pearls and precious stones of varied color and brilliance. "These things can't satisfy hunger," he thought. "They aren't worth as much as a meat bone. What good are they to a farm laborer?" So he shook his head.

The maidens implored him to take something. After deliberating he chose a shiny, blue stone rod lying in a corner of the cave. "Maybe this can be used as a salt grinder. It's just what we need." He thereupon placed it close to his bosom and left the cave.

Not far from the cave he again met the same old woman resting by the roadside. Looking at his bulging dress, she remarked, "Young fellow, you are lucky. Now you won't starve anymore."

The sight of the old woman reminded him of his mother waiting for whatever he brought. But the meat bone was gone. Ti Ti answered with a little grunt, "Humph, this is only a stone. There's no more meat bone."

"Young fellow, don't regret it. You've acquired a treasure." She then told him the secret of the stone rod and taught him how to use it.

This sent Ti Ti scurrying home. Placing the stone rod on a table, he anxiously tried knocking seven times and said, *"Come salt, come out salt."* Salt instantly gushed from the rod. When two buckets were filled, he knocked on the rod again and ordered, "Stop grinding. Stop!" And the salt came to a halt.

From far and near people spoke about the magic stone that Ti Ti and his mother possessed.

One day while Ti Ti was working in the fields, Ko Ko suddenly found time to return home. Dismounting from his carriage, he went into the hut where he greeted his mother. "I've come home especially to visit you, mother, and meanwhile see our family stone rod. I heard that it produces salt. Perhaps it's a genuine treasure."

Carefully taking the stone rod to show her son, she answered happily, "Yes, my son, this is really a treasure. Just give seven knocks and call out, *'Come salt, come out salt,'* and salt gushes from it."

"Our official household can't buy salt anywhere these days. Let me use it for a few days," he begged. "I'll come in person to return it and also bring some money from the salt I'll sell." Not waiting for an answer he snatched the stone rod and left as swiftly as he had come.

The next morning he bought a big boat and sailed for another land where he knew he could sell the salt at a big profit. When the boat reached the sea, the elder brother anxiously took the stone rod to examine it and thought, "I've not tried it yet." Laying it down on a plank he gave seven hard knocks, and mumbled, *"Come salt, come out salt.."* Thereupon salt gushed from the rod. The sight made him giddy. His eyes were glued on the rising salt that poured forth ceaselessly, covering his ankles, and then his thighs and filling the boat. Only then did he recover from his daze. He implored the stone rod to stop. But the stone rod was buried beneath the salt. Besides, he had not learned the magic words to make it stop. All he could do was shriek at the top of his voice, "Too much now, too much now! Come the next time!"

The boatmen jumped overboard to save themselves. Soon the official was buried with the salt that filled the boat to overflowing, and when the water began to flood the boat, it sank. The official, the stone rod and salt were buried in the sea, and that was the end of his greedy dream. But the rod kept on pouring salt, ceaselessly and endlessly, and that is how the sea became salty.

# The Silkworm

*A Han Folktale*

According to legend, Lei Tsu the wife of the Yellow Emperor, Huang Ti, discovered how to raise silkworms. The invention of sericulture, the production of raw silk, was also attributed to her.

During the Han Dynasty, caravans traveled via the Silk Road along the Tarim basin in the (present) autonomous regions of Sinkiang Province with all manner of precious wares for Asia where they were shipped to the Roman Empire, and vice versa. This was only a few decades after the death of Christ and was of great historical importance. It brought not only trade but cultural exchange between the Western world and the Celestial Empire. From the land of silk, Serica, as the Romans called China, came silks, as fine and delicate and transparent as a dragonfly's wing, sought by the Romans for their own togas and beautiful clothing for their wives. Cleopatra was said to have matched her dazzling beauty with the sumptuous silks spun as by an Immortal.

Long, long ago during Huang Ti's time, there was a couple living in a village somewhere in the south. They had only one daughter but she was very clever and known for her filial devotion.

One day, the father was called away to fight a tribal war. When bad news of impending defeat reached the village, the mother and daughter prayed for his safe return. Many days passed but no news came of him. The mother was beside herself with worry. "Oh, my good man!" she cried. "If anything happened to you how could we two womenfolk carry on? Ai, if anyone can save my man's life and bring him back to us, I'd be willing to give my only beloved daughter to him in marriage."

Hearing her mother's wish, the daughter said with

113

deep emotion, "I promise to marry whomever can save my father's life."

A white horse in the stable heard the promises, and galloped straight to the battle front. The man was surrounded by the enemy when he saw his own horse galloping toward him, and jumped onto his back. The valiant horse rushed through the enemy line and carried the man safely home.

The mother and daughter were overjoyed and realized the horse had saved his life. But how could they reward a horse with their promises? They gradually felt there was no way except to forget it. But strange to say, the horse always neighed in a peculiar manner and often waited at the window of the daughter's room. The mother and father became very upset and discussed the unusual situation every day. They agreed it was not right to break their promises, yet how could their daughter marry a horse? "We can't allow the horse to go on stomping at the girl's window and neighing like crazy. What an abomination!"

To put an end to it, they had the horse destroyed, and the hide was dried in the sun. The girl was very sad when she heard what her parents had done, and went to the courtyard to see the hide. As she stood there recalling how the horse had saved her father's life, a sudden gust of wind came up, and sent sand and stones flying. It whirled round and round the horsehide which tumbled down and enveloped the girl. In an instant, she was blown into the sky.

The father ran hurriedly after the horsehide until he reached the foot of a mountain where the hide had dropped onto a boulder. But when he arrived, nothing could be found except a number of small white worms that raised their tiny heads to look at him. Alas! What could he do? He gathered them to bring home to his wife.

The unhappy mother looked curiously at the strange

white worms that seemed quite tame. Thinking of her daughter, she felt sympathetic, and fed them with tender mulberry leaves. After a time, they grew up and then stopped eating. The mother took some straw from the stable and gently placed a thin layer over them. They appeared to find comfort nesting amidst the straw. Each worm found its own corner and began to spin a thin, white, shiny shell around its body. Patiently and ceaselessly it labored for days until it was entirely embedded in a smooth cocoon. By then the worm was transformed into a motionless insect. In the springtime, the insect bit through the cocoon. Little white, fluffy wings grew on each insect that fluttered round to mate. A vast quantity of yellowish eggs, tiny as a sesame seed, came forth from the females, and by early summer, they were again the same shiny, white worms. Once more the cycle was repeated until the next spring.

At last, one day, someone very patiently unwound the cocoon and obtained a great length of glossy threads, thin as a spider's web but strong as a human hair. By and by, they were known as silk threads and the worm was called a silkworm.

Every village woman raised silkworms, and worwhipped the girl as the Silkworm Goddess. Many temples have a goddess seated on a white horse while she carries a bamboo tray of silkworms. People earnestly believed that offerings made to her brought success in raising the silkworm.

# The Princess' Veil

### A Chuang Folktale

This Chuang folktale revealed more than a slight influence of Han culture. The emphasis on the chieftain's lack of benevolence, and the virtuous princess were of Confucian derivation; so, too, was the humble behavior of the young man, his respect for the chieftain, and wish to serve to the best of his ability.

Just as the dragon was associated with the Chinese, so the phoenix was linked with the minorities. The earliest mention of the phoenix was its use as the tribal emblem of Ch'ih Yu, the leader of the southern tribes that included the Chuang. When the Chou Dynasty king was losing control over his kingdom, Confucius remarked that since the time of Yao, Shun and Yü (the Golden Age) and early Chou, no scribe had recorded the singing of the phoenix, and he sighed for he was really saying that there was no enlightened sovereign ruling to bring peace and happiness to the kingdom. The phoenix later became a symbol of peace and good government.

During the Han Dynasty all creatures were grouped into five classifications according to their importance. The dragon, designated a scaly creature, ranked first; the phoenix, a feathered creature, came second. In antiquity the phoenix was depicted somewhat like a vulture, grotesque and quite angular. It was often made into an abstract design. But during the Han Dynasty, artists conceived it more realistically, rhythmic and graceful, endowed with beauty and color. It ultimately became the female counterpart of the dragon, and was used as an imperial emblem to signify the empress.

A long time ago there was a chieftain who had an unusually lovely daughter named Ghurtashi. She was not only beautiful, but intelligent and expert in weaving. She was given a shuttle made by five thousand skilled carpenters, and at the tender age of eight, began to weave her head-veil by using a long, silk thread made from the cocoons of five thousand silkworms. By the time she was sixteen, her head-veil was ready to be taken off the loom. The chieftain then decided to select a young man for her to marry. But, among all the high officials and princes of his choice there was not one who pleased her.

"Then what type of young man do you like, my beloved daughter?" he asked.

"Whoever can understand the significance of my head-veil and guess what was in my heart, will be the one I'll marry, no matter who he is."

The chieftain thereupon issued a proclamation according to his daughter's wish:

*Regardless of station, be it prince, official or commoner, whoever can recognize the meaning of her veil and fathom what was in her heart, will be given the princess in marriage.*"

The veil and notice were hung on the palace door. The entire countryside was stirred by the news, and the palace abuzz with onlookers eager to win such a fortune. From morning to night, people came, but no one was able to guess the meaning.

A half year slipped by, and the anxious chieftain became more uneasy. "My good girl, your conditions are impossible," he complained. "Even your own father can't guess what was in your heart."

"Beloved father," the princess replied. "People only see the veil but don't realize that the answer lies right in the woven silk."

Ten days later a young fellow from the eastern side of the mountain came at midnight. After looking at the veil carefully, he took it down and proceeded to the palace. The chieftain had already retired, but as soon as he was told that a man had dared take the veil, he hurriedly arose from his bed, and asked impatiently, "Do you know the meaning of the veil? Do you know what the princess had in her heart? If you can't answer at once, I'll have you thrown into prison for your impudence."

The young man saluted the chieftain and replied, "My respected and beloved chieftain, the princess' veil has told me the story of her heart. This I know."

The chieftain was relieved to hear someone say exactly what his daughter had said, and hastily called her to question the youth.

"What is the meaning in my veil?" the princess Ghurtashi inquired.

"On the veil is a high mountain. On the mountain is a cave. In the cave is a five-colored phoenix. But there is a demon guarding it. You are saying that whoever can get the phoenix will win a great fortune."

"You have guessed rightly. Then can you get the phoenix?"

"If I didn't think so, I wouldn't dare take down your veil."

The chieftain was not feeling entirely pleased but nonetheless asked, "Young fellow, are you willing to go? Whatever you need I'll provide."

"I don't require anything except the red ruby on top of the princess' headdress on the left side of her hair," he answered modestly.

Thereupon the princess removed the ruby and gave it to the youth who instantly departed. He walked for three days and nights to the side of a very high mountain where he took out the ruby and uttered a prayer, "Oh, red ruby, I've placed my whole life in you. If you are truly precious, emit ten thousand feet of dazzling light."

After this prayer he climbed the hill without fear. When he had almost reached the cave, he saw a demon nodding at the entrance. The young fellow stopped short of twenty paces and placed the ruby in his outstretched palm. At the approach of human steps, the demon awoke and jumped toward the intruder. At that instant tens of thousands of brilliant red rays flashed from the red ruby so the demon could not open his eyes. The young man quickly seized the five-colored phoenix and bounded from the cave. Then he started his journey back to the palace.

"Here is the precious phoenix that can speak," the yough said, presenting it to the chieftain. "I'll now request permission to take your daughter home."

The chieftain hemmed and hawed for he had no intention of keeping his word. Actually the king regarded this commoner as unworthy of his daughter and wished nothing more than to be rid of him. Finally he said, "Your power is indeed remarkable. But you acquired the phoenix too easily. I have another task for you, somewhat more difficult. After that I'll let you marry the princess."

"Please tell me the task, my chieftain," the youth said very humbly.

"Within my palace are fifty ponds, all very filthy. If by early morning before the first prayer, you can make them crystal clear so I can see to the bottom, you will be granted my daughter."

"Just as you command," the youth replied. He really saw through the chieftain's wiles, so without any further comment, he abruptly walked away. Yet he was not discouraged and instantly went to the imperial gardens to have a look at the ponds. True, they were as the chieftain had described. But how could he outwit the chieftain? As he was trying to figure a way, the princess appeared.

"Please don't worry," Ghurtashi said as she took a green emerald from the right corner of her headdress. "Take this precious stone, dip it once in all fifty ponds and the waters will instantly become clear as crystal."

The happy youth did as the princess suggested and in a twinkling, all the ponds sparkled. When the chieftain received an official report that the task had been accomplished, he was very angry. Thereupon an order was given for the youth to appear before the chieftain who began to rattle off a string of unreasonable demands: "In my garden are grapevines not yet ripe that I wish to eat right away. Make this possible. I have bolts of silk and numerous pieces of embroidery. Make them into beautiful clothing without using any thread. I have a hundred court ladies. Transform them into men. My beard is white and long. Make me as young as you. All these things must be completed within three days, otherwise, I'll have you beheaded."

The young man left without any reply.

Taking the youth by the hand, the princess said, "It is time to leave. Let's go." She took her veil and the five-colored phoenix and rode away on horseback accompanied by the brave youth. They had traveled only a hundred *li* when the chieftain with a large troop of soldiers caught up with the couple.

"My beloved daughter, how can you have the heart to leave your father but be willing to follow this poor, ordinary fellow? Follow me back to the palace immediately and I'll find a high official to become your husband."

He ordered the soldiers to seize the young man, but the princess commanded them to stop. Placing the bird on the ground, she turned to her father and said, "The most unhappy event in the world, is not our departure, but your lack of benevolence and your own failure to keep your word.

The princess and the young man then mounted the back of the five-colored phoenix and flew straight up to the sky. The angry chieftain instantly ordered his soldiers to shoot arrows at them, and give chase. But the princess spread out her veil thereby making herself and the youth invisible to the soldiers.

Princess Ghurtashi and the youth she had chosen as her husband, lived happily together forever.

# The One-Horned Ox

*A Yao Folktale*

The Yao people live in Kwangtung, Kwangsi and Hunan Provinces. In days of old, the Yao were virtually paupers. To be able to possess an ox would have been an unthinkable luxury that few if any, could afford. This story was merely wishful thinking, and a protest that revealed the unhappy relations between those in power and the common folk.

There are any number of tales about the revered but feared tiger. The speed of his descent from a high point of vantage, gave rise to the legendary flying tiger. During the Sino-Japanese War, the American air force commander, General Chennault organized a group in China, called the Flying Tigers, who were famous for their daring exploits. Later a cargo airline was developed by this same group and still operates today.

There was once a young man who lived amidst high mountains where he tilled a few patches of land for a living. But what he really liked to do more than anything else, was to draw. He would pick banana leaves, and by burning pine branches, make charcoal to draw on them whenever he had spare time. Thus, after a year, he was quite an accomplished artist.

Tilling the ground was hard work because he did not own an ox and had to depend solely on his simple spade and youthful energy. He would often go to a nearby village where people had oxen, pat the back of one, hold its tail with longing and murmur, "If I had an ox, how good, how good!"

One day when he returned he drew a very big ox with a single horn, and hung the picture on the wall in his

room. Every day, he spoke to the picture and said. "Good ox, come down to be my companion. If we could till the fields together, how nice it would be!"

Early one morning, he noticed a dark, shiny ox with only one horn, grazing in front of his hut and thought, "Now where could that have come from?" The ox came over to lick his hand and mooed in such a friendly manner. The youth hurriedly went to look at his drawing on the wall. Stange! The ox had disappeared. Only the banana leaf was still there. Then he realized that the one-

123

horned ox had walked down from his drawing, and he jumped up and down with joy.

During the day he tilled the ground with the ox. During the rest hours he played and rolled on the ground together with the ox, and in the night they slept in the same room. Every morning he would carefully place a fresh pile of soft hay beside it. He would eat admiring the ox, sleep with his hand on the ox, and whenever it made any noise, laugh with happiness.

Alas! One day the chieftain of his village passed by, noticed the shiny, one-horned animal in the field, and thought to himself, "The meat of that ox must be very tasty." Thereupon he ordered his soldiers to take it. The youth wept and begged the chieftain not to take the pleasure of his life away, but was ignored, and the ox was lead to the chieftain's mansion. The youth followed all the way to the gates where he begged the guards, "Please return my one-horned ox. He is my life." But the soldiers used a stick to beat him soundly. In a short time an ox horn and bone were flung from the house. The young man gathered the horn and bone of his beloved ox, and went home weeping uncontrollably.

He hung the horn on the wall where the drawing had been, and making a small mound, buried the bone in front of his hut. After two days a bamboo grew out of the mound. When the wind blew there was a very pleasing sound. It shot up ten feet at a time, growing taller and taller until it reached all the way to the heavens. He could hardly wait to see what was there. So the curious youth quickly climbed up the bamboo with his hands and feet moving like a frog. Up, up and up, he went through cottony, white clouds until he finally reached the top. How beautiful heaven was! Flowers of the five ancient colors (red, yellow, blue or green, black and white) were scattered in profusion over soft meadows. Fairies of great beauty were dancing in groups and singing. He stared as if bewitched, and silently watched them, lost in admiration. One fairy in particular was so beautiful he could not take his eyes from her.

"E-ee!" the fairies exclaimed in a startled voice as they caught sight of him.

A fragrant breeze blew over him. The meadows and fairies were instantly gone; only a blanket of white cloud remained. He sat on top of the bamboo that gradually began to shrink until it reached the ground and penetrated the mound, disappearing completely. "If only I could marry one of the fairies," he mused as he stared at the mound. But how could he ascend without the bamboo?

From morning to night, he dreamed about the fairies. He could not eat or sleep, and constantly stood in front of his hut to gaze at the sky. But one night, he had a dream wherein the one-horned ox spoke to him and said, "Little brother, have you forgot that you can make pictures? Draw a fairy on a banana leaf. Then grind the point of my horn until it has a hole; then blow through it, and the fairy of your choice will appear."

On awakening, he chided himself for not remembering that he could draw, and he set out for the mountainside to pick an extra large leaf. Using a pine branch to make some charcoal, he began to draw. He spent ten days drawing a fairy. But she was truly beautiful, just like the one in heaven who had enchanted him above all the others. After that he ground the point of the ox horn until a hole was visible, and then blew on it, "Toot, toot." A fragrant breeze arose, and a fairy came down from the banana leaf. The entire room was illuminated with a rosy hue.

"Little brother," the fairy said as she smiled. "You can till the ground; I can weave. Let us work together diligently."

Now, more than ever, he wished for an ox to till the

fields; so he promptly drew one on the banana leaf. **Then** he blew on his ox horn—"Toot, toot."

"Moo, moo," the ox said as it descended from the leaf. From then on, the young man tilled the ground together with the ox, and the fairy wove so deftly, that there was always enough to eat, and warm dress to wear. Thus they lived a sweet, happy life together.

But one day, the chieftain again happened to pass their way, and was quickly attracted by the beauty of the fairy. Soldiers were promptly ordered to carry her off to his mansion. The young husband followed them all the way to the gates where the guards began to beat him, just as before!

The unhappy man returned home in despair. What should he do to regain his fairy wife? After brooding over the matter, he recalled the banana leaf and his ox horn. So he ceased moping and went in search of the biggest leaf that he could find. He thereupon drew a winged tiger, and then blew on his horn, "Toot, toot . . . ," and a tiger instantly flew down.

"Oh, my brother tiger, let us fly to the chieftain's mansion to rescue the fairy," he said as he sat astride the tiger's back.

The tiger spread his wings and swiftly flew where the treacherous chieftain kept the lovely fairy. They could see the chieftain trying to persuade the fairy to become his wife. The young fellow dashed in with the tiger. All the soldiers and guards, their faces blue from fright, hid behind the screens. Then the tiger stooped down for the fairy to mount, and spread his wings to carry the fairy and her husband back to the mountains.

Thereafter, the man tilled the fields, and the fairy did her weaving. They lived a happy, contented life together in the mountains that later became known as the Ox Horn Range. One of the large mountains was named the Flying Tiger Mountain.

# Maiden Liu, the Songster

*A Yao Folktale*

Liu San Mei, a Han maiden, lived near the Kwangtung, Kwangsi border in the area known as Seven Star Cliff, which today is a scenic, provincial park. She was a dauntless character who protested at every turn the way that the Yao people were treated by the Han. Dignitaries as well as petty officials were ever conscious of the popular support that she received from the common people, and feared her ability to incite the large Yao tribe to revolt.

There is a traditional belief that Liu San Mei was the originator of folksongs in southern China. The songs exposed the evils of the ruling powers and were often sung to taunt the Han oppressors. People living in the border regions of Kwangtung and Kwangsi Provinces told many stories about Maiden Liu. This was one of the favorite tales from Kwangsi that showed how she stood up to a Han official, and defeated an old scholar by her wit.

Maiden Liu's derision of the old scholar and her attitude toward the classics, were not unique even though scholars and classical learning were revered throughout ancient history.

There were others during these times who believed it folly to study the classics, or use archaic thought and methods to rule their kingdoms, and sought to replace them by new ideas. Similar motives impelled the Ch'in emperor, Shih Huang to destroy the ancient classics and get rid of stubborn scholars.

Although the Yao had a hard life, they were a diligent, genial folk who loved to sing and dance, and had unusual talent in the field of music. Their musical compositions are indescribably beautiful.

In antiquity the Seven Star Cliff in the Kao Yao district had no human habitation. Only fierce animals roamed about the wild countryside until the Yao tribe migrated there. Then they bravely subdued the animals, got rid of the snakes and diligently planted crops on the hilltops. The people lived a very simple life. They liked to sing and dance, and gradually became known for these talents. The happy love songs of the young people reverberated throughout the mountain valleys. During their festivities, flutes and drums mingled with their singing and the dances often lasted from dusk to dawn. However, life was hard for them, and to make matters worse, the Yao did not get along with the Han officials. The Han armies were often sent to oppress them; soldiers burned their villages, and plundered the cows and sheep. There were many misunderstandings, so the Yao people just kept to themselves.

There was a Han maiden named Liu San Mei, living nearby the Yao villages. She was a farmer's daughter, compassionate, brave and beautiful. Her hair was dressed in a topknot resembling a curled cloud. She had shiny red cheeks and dark, sparkling eyes that looked like two drops of morning dew on a lotus leaf. Besides, she was an expert songster, and her name was known to the country-folk far and near.

She once organized an open singing contest that brought people from all parts of the countryside. Some traveled several days and nights to get there. As was customary, she sang in verse and then a participant rapidly replied. Whoever could remain singing the longest was

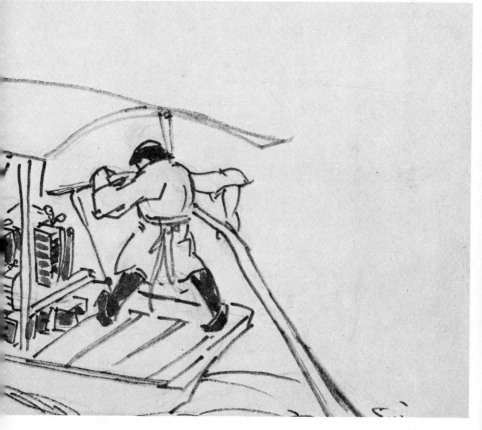

the winner. One by one, competitors dropped out, unable to cope with her endless repartee. She seemed to have a veritable spring of fresh songs that came from her heart.

An elderly scholar, well-known for his profound knowledge of the classics heard about her, and said with disdain, "This girl is only a village maiden. She could not have studied the classics or books of song. Who is she anyway?" He decided to challenge her, and shame her into silence. Hiring a boat that he loaded with classic books of song, he headed for her place. When he reached the village, he saw a lovely young girl washing laundry by the bank of the river. "Call your Maiden Liu here. I am a scholar who has come with a boatload of books to compete with her," he announced proudly.

The old scholar in the boat piled high with books was a comical sight to Liu San Mei who answered by singing in a vibrant voice,

> *Washing laundry at the riverside,*
> *is Liu San Mei.*
> *Sing your mountain songs,*
> *if you have any to come,*
> *For mountain songs*
> *come only from the heart.*
> *Whoever heard of songs laden in a boat,*
> *by river to come?*

The old scholar realized that she was the maiden he sought. He had come to expose her lack of knowledge and now she was poking fun at him! He was very upset as he tried to recall her song. Hurriedly he began opening his books to find the source, for he believed all songs could be traced to the classics. Laughter and insulting remarks came from the crowd that had gathered along the bank when he failed to find her verse. They stood half the morning without hearing him utter a single verse. The old scholar was so humiliated, he ordered the boatmen to turn around and shove off.

Everyone throughout the countryside heard what had happened, and respected Maiden Liu more than ever. She loved to sing the songs of the Yao tribe and even learned their dialect. She was truly loved by the Yao people who asked her to compose many songs for their tribe. When the Yao maidens sang their love songs during the spring festival, this one was always heard:

*How learned our Liu San Mei!*
*Gifted in singing and composing songs.*
*The songs, she composed*
*Handed down to posterity.*
*Just mention her name*
*Our hearts too, burst with song.*

The tales of Maiden Liu spread from one person to ten, from ten to a hundred until they reached the ears of the magistrate. He strongly condemned her behavior and pronounced her singing immoral.

Then one day while Liu San Mei was working in the fields, a group of young men saw her and began to compete with her in song. One verse was answered by the other's until the whole valley echoed with their songs. People stopped to listen, unable to tear themselves away. Pathways were blocked by young and old who tarried to enjoy the wit and ability of Liu San Mei.

It so happened that the magistrate was being carried through in his sedan chair, but despite the shouts of his chair-bearers, they could not pass. The magistrate stepped down and angrily ordered the maiden to cease singing. He scolded her roundly saying, "Study the classics and sing proper songs. A dutiful maiden doesn't go about stirring up trouble."

Breaking into song, she answered lightheartedly,

*When rooster crows, he pats his chest;*
*I sing to lighten my heart.*
*Stuffed with classics, mute in song,*
*Like covering a lantern with cowhide.*

Having no suitable rebuke, the magistrate mounted his chair and ordered his men to retreat.

The Han officials not only hated her songs, they were dissatisfied with her friendship with the Yao, and tried to think of ways to destroy it. But the brave maiden overcame all obstacles. She traveled throughout the countryside where she was welcomed by the Yao, and treated as one of them.

By and by she met a young man from the White Crane Cave district of the Yao tribe. He was a diligent cowherd and a talented singer. Whenever he sang, his rich, warm voice touched the inner springs of her heart. She would burst into song to express her admiration, and they became close, beloved companions.

At one of the annual Yao festivals when drums were beaten and cymbals clashed in the villages gaily festooned with myriads of decorations, the young men wearing new dress and a beautiful bird's feather in their turbans, came together with the maidens who likewise put on their best embroidered blouses and skirts, and wrapped their legs to endure long hours of dancing. They assembled at dusk near Seven Star Cliff to sing to their hearts' content. As evening wore on people noticed in the moonlight, the silhouette of a young man and a maiden on top of the cliff. Maiden Liu and her lover could be clearly recognized. The most melodious songs ever heard, drifted from the clifftop like a crystal waterfall. Countless people listened to their singing which continued for seven days and nights. Finally, admist the most melodious song, the couple was transformed into stone images. It was said that they became Celestial Spirits.

Her stone image and an altar for people to worship the maiden are still in the waterfall cave of the Seven Star Cliff. Every year during the spring festival, multitudes visit the cave to pay homage to the beloved songster. Many folk worship her as a Goddess Protector of Crops.

Cowherds around the Seven Star Cliff area still sing this ballad—

> *Liu San Mei,*
> *Send us the wind.*
> *Where is the wind?*
> *In the Yellow Weed forest.*
> *Push away the Yellow Weed;*
> *Let the wind pass.*

The Yao people protected themselves by concealing their true thoughts from the Han officials. Wind stood for freedom. The Yellow Weed was a derogatory term for the hated Han oppressor. Yellow was the Chinese imperial color, and used when issuing orders that were written on yellow paper or cloth.

> *You give the sun,*
> *I, the crop;*
> *I give the mountain valley*
> *For your herd to roam.*

In the last stanza, the sun was symbolic of man, the male principle. Woman produced the crops, the growth-children. Woman gave as the mountain valley for the cowherd to be nourished and his tribe to increase.

Liu San Mei possessed spirit and courage. She dared to fight for freedom on behalf of the Yao people. In fact, she stood as a symbol of friendship between the Yao and Han. Although she was a Han, she rebelled against the oppressions of the Han rulers. Her songs are eternal, remembered by all.

# The Ten Thousand Treasure Mountain

*A Yao folktale*

Ten thousand, once considered an extremely high figure, had an added dimension signifying limitless or countless. *Wan Shui*, meaning ten thousand years, was used in antiquity, as a greeting on the New Year to wish the emperor long life. With the founding of the Chinese Republic in 1912 this fell into disuse; then about two decades ago the expression was again revived to wish Chairman Mao Tse-tung longevity and innumerable years of happiness. But after the Cultural Revolution, it was again discontinued. This Yao tale used ten thousand to signify the myriad treasures within a mountain cave.

The picturesque, often spectacular landscape with amazing shaped mountains and caves in Kwangsi, in the northern part of Kwangtung, and near the Kweichow border in the southern and western part of Hunan, where the Yao people dwell, was often the setting for imaginative folktales. Chinese artists depicted them quite realistically although they appear fantastic and imaginary to those who have never visited these regions.

The gold and silver found in the mountain areas were made into all kinds of ornaments and jewelry. The Yao women liked to adorn themselves with very large loops of silver necklaces, earrings, bracelets and hair ornaments—as today.

Deep in a valley amidst high mountains there once lived an old woman and her son named K'o-li. Every day he went to the mountains to dig the roots of the turtle foot plant. Beating the roots to shreds, rubbing and sieving them in a large wooden drum filled with water, the white starchy powder settled at the bottom. This was steamed and used as a staple since they were far too poor

to have rice or corn. But one day K'o-li had a sore foot that prevented him from digging more than a small amount. Now there would be only a small bowl of the powder for their meal!

"Mother, you eat it," the unselfish boy said. "I'm not hungry."

"My child, you eat it," the kindly mother replied. "I don't feel hungry either."

As the mother and son were urging each other to eat the pitifully small bowl of powder, an old man with a long, white beard appeared outside the door. He was so pale looking, and seemed so feeble and shaky. Holding a peculiar walking stick to support himself, he leaned against the door.

"Old man, you must be starved," the mother called out.

The beggar nodded without saying a word.

"My child, you don't feel like eating nor do I. Let us give this to the old father."

K'o-li instantly handed the food to the old man who finished it in a few mouthfuls. Then he made a gesture indicating that he wished to go home.

"Old father," K'o-li said as he brought out a large basket, "Let me carry you home."

The old man nodded again, and K'o-li helped him into the basket, strapped it over his shoulders and set out in the direction where the old man's fingers pointed.

K'o-li walked through a forest, crossed deep gorges and climbed mountain slopes until they reached a big stone cave under a cliff. A lovely maiden hurriedly came forth to welcome the old man and exclaimed, "Old father, you have come back!"

The old man jumped out of the basket and greeted the maiden *Mi-mi*. All of a sudden he could speak! "This young man is truly wonderful! Take off your earrings and make them into keys so he can open the mountains to get some treasures."

The maiden immediately removed a gold earring from her right ear and a silver one from her left ear, hammered one into a golden key and the other into a silver key. Giving them to K'o-li, she said, "Young brother, on the right side of this mountain there is a Ten Thousand Treasure Mountain. In the saddle of the mountain is a big stone cave called Ten Thousand Treasure Cave. You will see a big yellow stone just like a door at the entrance. Put the golden key into the tiny hole in the stone, and it will open. Within are countless treasures that you may take according to your heart's desire. The stone door will automatically close as soon as you have entered the cave. When you wish to come out, use the silver key by inserting it into a tiny hole at the back of the door. Take care not to lose the silver key or you won't be able to get out again."

"How can I take your earrings?" K'o-li asked with concern.

"Hurry! Go now," the old man shouted. "A tiger is coming to eat you up."

K'o-li looked around but saw no sign of any tiger. At that instant the old man took the maiden by the hand and went into the stone cave. A large stone dropped down fitting snugly into the cave entrance. Only a pair of shiny keys were left lying at his feet, and all around was quiet.

At last K'o-li picked up the keys and wandered home to relate what had happened. His mother listened thoughtfully and said, "My child, we dig turtle foot roots day after day just to get a little of the pulp. That is really not the way to live. See what implements are in the cave. If you bring something to help us farm, that won't be a bad idea."

K'o-li took the keys and went to the Ten Thousand Treasure Mountain where he found the stone cave with the yellow stone door sealing the entrance. He entered by using the golden key and the door closed behind him with a BANG. K'o-li saw countless treasures, precious pearls, silver and gold objects. He looked east, west, and all around. The dazzle and sparkle confused him, and for a long time, he wondered what to take home. Then he recalled his mother's suggestion and decided to pick an implement. "There, that white stone grinder lying in the corner—I'll take that home to earn my living by grinding grains. That will be good," he thought as he took the grinder. He then inserted the silver key as the maiden had instructed, and the door opened instantly. When he walked out of the cave, the door closed behind him with a BANG. The lad then went happily homeward.

His mother put the white stone grinder in the middle of the room and turned the stone lid a few times to see how it worked. Many grains of corn suddenly rolled out. The more they turned, the more rolled out until corn spilled all over the ground. The old mother and her son laughed with joy until their jaws ached. "How can the two of us ever finish all this? Let us give some to poor people," she finally said. So K'o-li filled a large basket to the very top with grains and distributed them among the neighbors. Everyday the stone grinder turned out grains of corn, and each day some were given away.

It was not long before the story of the white stone grinder reached the ears of the king who immediately sent a high official with troops of soldiers to K'o-li's house. Off went the stone grinder to the palace. The happy king walked over to feel the grinder. With just one touch—*si-sa,* it turned into a pile of white lime. The king was so furious, his face turned blue. "Behead that useless official!" he ordered the soldiers.

The old mother was very upset, and asked, "My son, do you still have the keys?"

"Yes, I'm carrying them close to my breast," he replied.

"Then return to The Ten Thousand Treasure Mountain and find something else," she urged K'o-li.

K'o-li went back and this time took a yellow stone mortar. They tried using it by pounding with a wooden pestle, and pearly white rice instantly fell out! The more they pounded, the more fell out!

The story soon reached the king who once again dispatched soldiers together with a high official to take away the stone mortar. The happy king walked over to examine it, but this time took care to feel it very gently. Yet with just one touch—*si-sa,* the stone mortar turned into a heap of yellow clay. The king was so enraged, even his beard bristled, and he shouted to his soldiers, "Behead that useless official!"

Once again K'o-li returned to the Ten Thousand Treasure Cave and this time brought back a hoe. He moved the hoe merely once over the barren ground in front of their hut, and strange to say, a great big cornstalk having many giant ears of corn instantly shot up. He moved it back and forth ten times, and ten giant cornstalks shot up; then a hundred times, and one hundred cornstalks shot up, then . . . . Again, mother and son were overcome with laughter. K'o-li, once more gave a generous amount to the neighbors. Soon everyone was talking about the magic hoe, and, of course, the news reached the king who said, "This time we are not going to take away the hoe. So far everything has turned to either lime or clay. Bring the young fellow here for questioning."

Thus a high official with soldiers went to K'o-li's house where he was bound hand and foot and carried to the

palace. The king sat on his throne flanked by executioners with axes and knives. "Where did your treasures
come from? Speak out," the vicious king commanded,
"and you will be rewarded. Otherwise I'll have you
beheaded."

The executioners shouted in unison to threaten K'o-li.
But why should he be afraid? He remained silent but
racked his brains for the best way to keep the secret. All
of a sudden it dawned on him and he replied, "My
treasures were obtained from the Ten Thousand
Treasure Cave in the Ten Thousand Treasure Mountain.
There is so much treasure there, it is endless."

The king laughed aloud with happiness and said,
"Very good, we will go to take it all. Give me the key at
once. Take the lead and guide us there."

The king was born aloft in his sedan chair accompanied by troops who carried huge empty baskets while
K'o-li guided them. On their arrival the king took out the
golden key from his vest, rushed into the cave, followed
by all his soldiers, officials and attendants. 'BANG,' the
stone door closed behind them.

"King, you wicked one!" K'o-li shouted from without.
"The silver key is in my hand. Stay in the cave forever!"

K'o-li hurried home to tell his mother what had
happened. "You are a clever, good son," she said
thankfully. "We still have the hoe so let us till the land
for corn."

"Ma-ma, the maiden Mi-mi, gave me two keys,"
K'o-li said in dismay as he suddenly remembered that
there was now only a silver one. "What can I do? They
are her earrings."

"I'll go with you to return it and we can apologize for
the loss," she replied.

Mother and son each carried a basketful of corn on
their shoulders. They passed through the forest, crossed

the deep gorge and climbed the mountain slopes until they saw the old father, his long, white beard swaying gently in the breeze, and his granddaughter sitting at the entrance of the stone cave.

"I'm so sorry that the golden key was lost," K'o-li said as he returned the silver one. A soft rosy hue spread over her face as she silently took the key. She twisted it back into an earring, and placed it in her left earlobe.

The mother said, "Old father, here are two baskets of corn. They are really not much more than a taste, but it is all from your precious hoe."

"Old woman, I don't need your corn. Better keep it for the poor people. Your son is honest and diligent so I'll give my granddaughter to him in marriage." As soon as he finished talking, he walked into the cave. A big stone door dropped, sealing the cave entrance, and the maiden was left behind. The old woman looked tenderly at the lovely young maiden, then at her beloved, strong son. She took one hand of her daughter-in-law, and the other of her son, and smiling, went home.

# The Golden Carp

*A Uighur Folktale*

The words *fish* (yü) and *abundance* (yü) have the same sound thus making *fish* a rebus for *wealth*, although their written characters are entirely different. The fish has a long tradition of symbolizing good luck, wealth and happiness. The carp was used to represent these sentiments. Therefore, the carp was a popular subject for New Year paintings, or wedding gifts. Money lenders used the carp for the same symbolic reasons. Writing paper employed carp for a decorative effect, but it also signified a letter.

The carp in this folktale that assumed the form of a young man to repay the kindness of the little boy, provided an age-old lesson found in many a western tale; the innocent child succeeded whereas the greedy fisherman failed. The background of this folktale was the desert country of the northwest where the carp was considered valuable because of its rarity.

One day a man caught a golden carp of rare beauty. He laughed with happiness as he stretched to take the fish out of the net. But the carp unexpectedly leapt into the air, and slipped into the river again. He was so sad about the incident that thereafter, he went to fish at the same place, day after day. Although he caught many other fish, there was no sign of the glistening, golden fish. Three years later, having earned enough money as a fisherman, he decided to become a merchant. Yet he never forgot the glistening, golden carp.

When his wife died he eventually married a widow who already had a little boy. One day, after watching people fish in the river, the child asked his mother if he too could fish with a net that he had seen in their home. "You are too young; besides it is far too dangerous," she replied with concern. But the boy had a will of his own, and in the end, she yielded to his wish.

He was happy as could be, as he set out for the river. Once there, he cast his net and sat down to wait. After a while, the net seemed heavy, so he gleefully pulled it up. Within was a large golden carp! He cradled the long fish in both hands. Oh, such a gleaming fish! Never had he seen one like it. Packing his things quickly, he set out for home. He walked along for quite a few paces but then stopped to deliberate, "Should I sell it or eat it?" He fondled the fish most tenderly and murmured, "It's a pity to eat you—you brilliant, golden fish. I better let you go back to the water." So he went all the way back to put the fish into the water. Feeling satisfied, he skipped gaily home with nothing except his empty net.

Some neighbor children had seen him catch the fish and let it go free. "What a queer thing to do!" they thought, and ran to his father's shop to tell him about it. Although the merchant had liked the little boy at first, they had become estranged, and after a time, he no longer liked the child. But now, his hatred and anger mounted. For eight years he had been dreaming about the golden carp. His step-son had actually caught the fish and let it go! "If I had the golden carp, I'd be very rich," he muttered. He went home, and confronting his step-son, demanded, "Who told you to free my golden carp?" He grabbed his sword, threatening to kill the child, who was so terrified he shrank back from the furious step-father, and could not utter a word. "That golden carp is more precious to me than a step-son like you," the father shouted in a rage.

"How can you be so cruel to kill him for just one fish?" his wife sobbed. After seeing how hopeless it was to reason with him she said, "Even if you want to kill the child, you can't do it in broad daylight. Wait until night falls, then no one will know." The father left in a huff, and the lad was not harmed for the time.

Mother and son embraced and wept. Finally, she wiped her tears and said, "My son, you must leave. You can't stay here with your mother any longer." Thereupon she gave him a bag of food, and counseled him, "If you find a companion along the road, always test his sincerity by saying that you have to go into the bushes. If he is willing to wait, he will be a good companion. Otherwise, don't trust him. He will more than likely take advantage of you." With that, her son departed.

Somewhere along the road he met a man and the two walked together for half a day. At last he asked the fellow to wait for a few minutes while he went into the bushes. When he returned the man had already gone. The next day he again tested a fellow traveler this way and he likewise disappeared. So it seemed that his mother was right. On the third day he traveled alone until the sun was setting when suddenly a big, strong, young man appeared on the right side of the road and without any hesitation said, "Little brother, let us walk together. Why are you walking alone?"

The boy honestly related that his father had wanted to kill him, but his kind mother sent him away. "But I don't really know where I'm going," he said dejectedly.

"Don't feel bad about it," he answered. "From now on wherever we go, we'll go together. I'll help you." They became good friends and in no time at all were just like real brothers.

After walking for two days, they reached a city where many delicious things to eat were displayed in the open and within shops. However, there was an age old custom, observed very strictly, to pay cash or forfeit one's life. Of course these two hungry fellows did not know that. Nevertheless, the young boy was anxious and said, "We don't have any money. How can we eat here?"

"What is there to be afraid of? We can work instead of paying."

With that they entered a shop and ate until satisfied. When the bill came, since neither could pay, they volunteered to do whatever work was required.

"Certainly not!" the owner said, and instantly sent a petition to the chieftain demanding punishment for them.

"How dare you disobey my laws?" the chieftain called out in a stern voice, as the two men stood before him. Without waiting for an explanation, he said, "You have deceived us and that is punishable by death." An order was given to have them hanged.

A counselor arose requesting a few words with the chieftain, who was willing to listen. "It is my humble opinion," he said, "that these two youths should be sent to rescue your daughter who was taken away by the demon. Seven years have now passed and all the men sent so far have never returned. These two are very strong and don't seem like cowards. If they succeed, they can be rewarded with worthy posts, and your daughter given to one in marriage. If they fail, it won't be too late for punishment."

The chieftain consented and even gave them his own saber and two of his favorite chestnut brown steeds. The men readily accepted the task and began the journey. After traveling for two days they came to a high mountain where there were steep cliffs and large boulders that forced them to dismount and proceed on foot.

"Did you notice anything?" the elder asked when they reached the mountaintop.

"Yes, I saw a golden house in the valley, a river on the right side of the house and a bridge in front of it."

As they were speaking, an old woman demon suddenly appeared. Her eyes were as large as rice bowls and her tongue protruded three feet from her mouth. "Who are you that dare come here to meet your end!" she shrieked. "You are only two, but even if you were two hundred or two thousand, you couldn't take the princess. Your chieftain has sent hundreds of thousands of cavaliers each year. The mountains that you now stand on are piled high with their bones," she said proudly, and added with scorn, "You little ones, you are still dripping with your mothers' milk. With one breath, I could scrape off all the flesh and spit your bones into the sky. I need only blow and you will become meat for my dinner. I . . . "

Without waiting for her to finish, the youth angrily pulled out his saber and started to thrust it at her. With a single breath, she blew it into the sky. Seeing his brother in danger, the elder one called out, "Little brother, step aside. Let me handle her."

"Very well," the demon sneered, "you can be the first to die."

In an instant, she blew in and out like a whirlwind. He let himself be sucked into her, and then swiftly jabbed his saber deep into her throat. Her head was immediately split in two. The two brothers were exceedingly jubilant.

As they were cleansing themselves and the saber at the riverside, a lovely maiden came along carrying a golden long-necked jug. "You powerful warriors!" the startled maiden cried. "Where did you come from? No ordinary mortal can reach here."

"The chieftain's daughter was carried off by a demon. We have come to rescue her and bring her back to the kingdom," they replied.

"Hurry, run!" she urged them. "If the demon catches sight of you, she will devour you. I am the chieftain's daughter. My father has sent so many cavaliers already. Unhappily, all have been swallowed by the demon."

"Princess, go to the back of the mountain and have a look."

The princess made haste to go, and to her amazement, saw the demon lying dead.

"You are really heroes!" she exclaimed. "But alas! There are still her two sons who have been gone forty days, and should return today."

"Princess, have no fear. We can surely defeat both these demons."

The princess happily lead them to the golden house where she served the most savory food and wine. After a while the elder brother said, "You protect the princess by standing guard in front of the house, while I hide under the bridge."

It was not long before the two demons—one white, the other black, came into sight. They could smell the presence of human beings afar and demanded, "Human beings! Who are you?"

Jumping from his hiding place, the elder brother shouted with all his might, "You demons, return the chieftain's daughter or I'll tear open your bellies and chop off your heads."

"You are like a newborn babe. You dare to talk so boldly! Come to meet your end," the white demon replied, and following that, lifted his long spear and thrust it straight toward the young man's heart. But the youth was unafraid, and taking hold of the spear, broke it in two.

The black demon was truly astonished and thought, "That spear can hold the weight of the mountains without breaking, yet this fierce fellow is getting the better of my brother. Let me handle him." He thereupon jumped like a madman, aiming at the young man with an iron sledge hammer weighing over three hundred *catties* and cried, "Look out for this one!"

Without flinching, the youth drew his saber to meet the hammer head-on, and with a single stroke, split it in two. He then grabbed both demons, chopped off their heads and hung them on top of the bridge. The youth rushed over to embrace his brother, and greatly elated, they started out with the princess on their fast steeds. After passing deserts, mountains and wild country, only another day's journey remained to reach the capital. They stopped overnight at a village where everyone came to welcome the princess and the two heroes. When the chieftain listened to the report brought by an old man, he was so happy, he rewarded the bearer of the good news with a plate of gold. The chieftain then set out with his counsellors. Four thousand cavaliers accompanied by musicians blowing pipes and beating drums, marched until they reached the village. Amidst great rejoicing, the princess and the two heroes were carried straight to the palace.

After seven days had elapsed, the chieftain announced that he would gladly consent to the marriage of the princess. Which of the two would it be? Each brother was willing to let the other marry the maiden. But at last, the elder one said, "Younger brother, you had better marry the princess. I can't have a wife. You will understand later."

Therewith the marriage celebrations began, and continued for many days.

"It is time for me to leave," the elder brother announced one day.

"If you go, I'll go with you," the youth replied.

The chieftain understood how sad his son-in-law was at the thought of parting from the elder brother, and tried to persuade the elder brother to stay. When he saw it was no use, he gave them choice food, gold and silver, and allowed his daughter to accompany them.

One day they came to a river whereupon the elder brother asked everyone to stop for a rest. Then turning to his younger brother, he said, "Brother, when you were a boy, you cast a net into this river. Did you catch anything?"

"Yes, a golden carp of rare beauty."

"What did you do with the carp?"

"I put it back into the river."

"Younger brother, you have a good heart. I am that carp. You treated me so well. Not wishing me to die, you set me free, and suffered great hardship because of me. Therefore, I came to repay you—such as it was. To be a friend when you had need of me. But now I must say farewell." Having spoken, he suddenly leapt into the river. In a while a brilliant golden carp swam over, nodded, and then swam away.

# The Ungrateful Ones

*A Han Folktale*

During the Warring States Period (Second and Third Century B.C.) the Chou king was rapidly becoming a titular sovereign. The ancient codes and rules were breaking down; ancestral worship, loyalty to the king, and fidelity to the family were passing into oblivion. Fourteen feudal states fought desperately to gain their objective: the hegemony. The vassals who controlled the states had become greedy for power. People were like grass to be mowed down if they stood in the way; cities were for burning to gain the end of the princes, dukes or lords. War, hunger and death continued unabated.. These problems have been with us for centuries though we often think of them as peculiar to our own world today.

It was during this chaotic period in China that the philosophers, Han Fei-tze, Mencius, Mo-tze and others emerged to advocate their ideas for a sane leadership and plead for a peaceful society. There were debates, similar to those held by the Greek philosophers, their contemporaries. Each philosopher believed he had the panacea for the ills of the age, and often denigrated the other's thought. Yet it was a flowering period for art, literature, science and philosophy. Many of the great thinkers used an animal as a metaphor to illustrate a point. This folktale was an example and specifically ridiculed Mo-tze's philosophy that advocated love for all mankind even if it involved self-sacrifice that was not warranted.

During the Warring States Period more than two thousand years ago, a wolf was loitering on a mud road leading to a country village. He was enjoying himself immensely when he suddenly heard the hoofs of a horse coming from behind. Turning his head, he saw a hunter galloping with a bow and arrow in his hand. The wolf quickened his pace and ran for dear life. After racing for some distance, he caught sight of an aged man carrying a sack of books on his back. The wolf knelt down and begged the man to save his life.

"How can I save your life?" the old man anxiously asked for he was a kindly scholar named Tung K'uoh, a follower of Mo-tze.

"Old scholar, aren't you carrying a sack of books?" the wolf replied. "Just empty it and let me hide inside. That's all that's necessary."

The compassionate old man hurriedly hid the wolf in his sack and slowly walked on. By this time the hunter had caught up with the scholar, asked a few questions, and finally rode away in search of the wolf.

No longer hearing any sound of hoofs, the wolf figured that the hunter must have left, so he called out, "The hunter has gone far away already. Let me out."

As soon as the scholar put the sack down, the impatient wolf jumped out and sprang at the old man.

"What is this all about?" Tung K'uoh asked.

The wolf laughed cunningly and then sneered, "Old Head, I've not eaten for three days. If I let you go I'll starve. You have done a good deed; now complete the deed by letting me eat you up."

Tung K'uoh was so flabbergasted, he just didn't know what to say. After a long argument, he said to the wolf, "Such an ungrateful creature! Never in all the world have I heard of such reasoning. Let us ask anybody and if he says that I should be eaten after having saved your life, I won't complain." So they agreed to walk together and find a third party to be the judge. But nobody appeared on the road even after a long time whereupon the wolf became impatient.

"There are some apricot trees across the road," Tung K'uoh suggested. "Let us ask that old one with the wise,

glistening eyes." Consequently they stopped by the tree and after relating the whole story, Tung K'uoh asked, "Old revered apricot tree, will you please give us your honorable opinion? Do be fair in your judgment."

After listening carefully, the old apricot tree laughed aloud and said, "Old scholar, I understand your plight. But let me tell you my own story: I am a very old apricot tree and have been supplying my master with delicious fruit for over ten years. With the money he earned by selling my apricots, he brought a house and got married. Besides, he often sat under the shade of my luxuriant foliage to enjoy a cool summer breeze. Now that I've grown old and can't bear fruit any longer, the master is going to chop me down for firewood. I overheard this only yesterday. Old scholar, can you imagine such a fate after all my good deeds? That is how the master rewards me! You saved only one life. Compare your deed with mine. There is certainly a big difference."

The wolf was very gleeful to hear this tale, but Tung K'uoh was most dissatisfied. "After all," he said, "a tree isn't the same as a living being. We must ask a being such as an animal."

The wolf was willing and so they continued along the road where they met an old ox. "Old fellow, hurry and ask the ox," the wolf urged. "Otherwise I'm going to gobble you up now."

But the old ox also had a mouthful of complaints and said, "In spite of my hard work in the fields, all my life serving the farmer, he's going to have me slaughtered soon."

The scholar was very upset and said excitedly, "Since we have already questioned two parties, we must ask a third one. That will really be final. If the same thing is said, I won't argue anymore."

As they traveled along the road, they met a kindly old

man with a long beard. Tung K'uoh instantly asked him to be the judge. But without waiting for the end of the scholar's story, the wolf interrupted saying, "Oh, fair old master, don't listen to his tale. When he lured me to jump into his sack, he was figuring that the hunter would have killed me anyway so he might as well finish me off himself. He tried to suffocate me by putting heavy books on me. You can see how black his heart is."

This really was the limit! The scholar became very angry.

But the long-bearded one merely smiled, combed his long white beard with his fingertips and replied, "Both of you have your own reasons, I'm sure. However, I wasn't there to see what actually happened. Now then, how did you jump into the sack? How did he press you with his load of books? Please, both of you—reenact the whole incident so that I can see for myself."

Thereupon Tung K'uoh quickly emptied his sack of books, and the wolf readily jumped into the sack. Tung K'uoh then covered the wolf with his books as before and placed the sack on his shoulder. He was just about to walk along when the bearded old man took out a small, sharp knife, handed it to Tung K'uoh and made a stabbing gesture. But although the old scholar held the knife, he began to tremble and hesitated. He was after all, an ardent follower of Mo-tze's philosophy.

"You are truly foolish and timid," the bearded one said in a cold voice. "Are you going to let the ungrateful wolf go free? You should know that if you don't kill him, he will kill you. Make haste, move your hand and do what you must."

And that was the end of the ungrateful wolf.

# A Bride for the River God

*A Han Folktale*

The use of divination to foretell events was initially practiced by the outside tribes known as 'southern barbarian,' but later adopted by the Chinese. Diviners have survived throughout history and even today are consulted by some to discover the location of water or minerals in the ground by using a divining rod.

The Shang kings were so dependent upon their diviners that nothing was ever decided until one or more had been consulted. The Shang were notorious for their superstitious beliefs and cruel practices. Yet there was one sovereign, Wu Yi, far in advance of his time who tried to prove the inherent absurdity of superstition, and thus discredit the diviners. The method he used, was to play some games to show that Heaven would not punish him: He played chess with an official who represented Heaven. Each time the sovereign won, he would take the official's dress and beat it. The official did not dare to win when playing with him; thus Heaven lost many times and received repeated beatings. However, the king died while out hunting one day, supposedly stricken by a thunderbolt. His enemies said that this was Heaven's punishment for Wu Yi's sacrilegious acts. After his death, the diviners regained their power. The struggle between the sovereign and diviners for power, weakened the dynastic rule.

The rulers of the Chou Dynasty made laws to break the practices of their predecessors, but the cruel superstitions lingered and were not easy to destroy.

People in the Yeh district of the Wei Kingdom were very superstitious, and unscrupulous people could easily take advantage of them. Diviners were especially powerful, and each year caused great sorrow to many a family.

"The River God must be appeased each year otherwise a flood will destroy the crops and everyone will perish," a

155

group of women diviners proclaimed. "The most beautiful maiden possible with a rich dowry must be sent to him."

When the chief diviner pointed her finger at anyone's daughter, she would be taken as a sacrifice for the River God. No one ever dared to refuse the diviner's command. An elaborate ritual was performed on the selected day, and the maiden, dressed in her finest raiment, was carried to the riverside and thrown into the river with her dowry. After the River God's appetite was appeased, the people were told, the diviners were the only ones privileged to recover anything from the river. Many lovely maidens were thus sacrificed and the diviners grew very rich.

One year a new magistrate named Si Men Pao arrived in the Yeh district. He was a scholar who earnestly wished to destroy all superstitious customs. Yet he pretended to believe in this one and said, "We must worship the spirits and gods. Next year I shall personally attend the ceremony for the River God." This was publicly announced, and made the diviners very happy since with his support their plunder would be even greater.

That year there was the biggest procession ever seen, and the new magistrate attended wearing his ceremonial robes. He observed that the maiden chosen to be sacrificed, looked so miserable, whereas the diviners were happy, laughing and chatting with one another. But Si Men Pao turned to the chief woman diviner and said, "This maiden is not at all beautiful. How could she ever qualify as a wife for the River God? Go down to the river and tell the River God to wait until we chose a more beautiful maiden. We will select another and send her to him."

Thereupon the magistrate ordered his petty officer to seize the diviner and throw her into the river. Using this same method, he had three more thrown into the river and drowned. He had every intention of continuing and so be rid of them all, thus finally breaking the cruel custom perpetuated by these women. But the others became fearful of their own lives and realizing that they could not deceive the magistrate as they had the populace, they knelt before him and confessed to their trickery.

"Aha! I thought that the River God really must have a maiden each year. Apparently, the whole custom was only fabricated by you diviners," Si Men Pao sneered.

He did not detain the women for any punishment, but scolded them and gave a long lecture on superstitions. Thereafter the River God did not need a maiden to be sacrificed. In fact, all the diviners had to change their work. Peace reigned in the Yeh district and there were no floods either.

# The Tibetan Envoy and the T'ang Dynasty Princess

*A Tibetan Folktale*

Throughout Chinese history, sovereigns have used varied tactics instead of warfare to contend with the outside tribes. One method was to have the emperor's daughter marry the chieftain of a hostile tribe. However, during the T'ang Dynasty although more amicable relations could have been achieved with the Tibetans in this way, the emperor was reluctant to have his daughter leave for a place so far from the northern capital. The incident related in this folktale had historic importance and the characters involved where real personages, T'ai Tsung being the T'ang ruler, Wen Ch'eng, his daughter, Ch'i Tsung Tsan Pu, the Tibetan envoy and Songtsan Gambo, the Tibetan chieftain.

There was once a T'ang Dynasty emperor who had a very lovely daughter. She was also a scholarly person and was therefore named Wen Ch'eng. (Wen meaning literary, and Ch'eng—accomplished). When the princess came of age the chieftains of seven neighboring kingdoms sent envoys to ask for her hand.

One of her admirers, a Tibetan chieftain, sent a most eminent person as his envoy. However, the emperor was really unwilling to have his daughter marry the chieftain in Tibet because he thought it entirely too far from the Middle Kingdom. Not only would he miss the company of this lovely daughter because of the distance from his own kingdom, but he was also concerned about the hardships she would have to endure. He knew the Tibetans were lacking in skilled craftsmen and carpenters, that they were lacking even in kinds of foods and creature comforts his daughter had been accustomed to all her life. He could not openly disclose his true feelings so he asked his most capable minister to find a suitable way of refusing and at the same time select a worthy suitor.

After a discussion they decided to hold a contest. Five hundred mares and an equal number of colts were gathered in the morning. The colts were placed in the center of a large compound surrounded by the mares. A proclamation was then issued:

*The seven neighboring chieftains are my trusted allies. I wish I had seven daughters for each of them. But since I have only one daughter worthy of her name, I do not know which suitor should be the chosen one. In order to be fair, a contest will be arranged. Your chieftain will be considered eligible if his honorable envoy can lead all five hundred colts to their own mothers and the five hundred mares recognize their colts.*

With that, six envoys started to work on the solution. One by one, the six were either kicked by the mares or the horses bolted. The colts also stayed away from the mares. Not one of the envoys could lead a colt to its mother, nor did any mare recognize her colt.

The seventh envoy, a Tibetan, had courteously stepped aside, and now it was his turn to try. Tibetans are instinctively good horse breeders and so, not following the clumsy methods of the others, he let the colts eat as much as they desired. After being satisfied they began to neigh, prance about and run to find their own mothers to suckle. The mares lowered their heads sniffing and urging their own colts to milk. Without any fuss, all five hundred mares were united with their colts.

Although the emperor was pleased with the clever performance, he was not happy about the outcome and said,

"The Tibetan envoy is clever and I am pleased. Yet, in order to be fair to all the others, there will be another contest. He then displayed a precious, translucent piece of green jade and said, "This piece of jade has a zigzag flaw, like a tunnel. Whoever can put a silk thread from one side through to the other, will be considered the successful envoy."

Once again all six worked very hard to solve the problem, but failed. Having worked the entire morning they finally handed it to the Tibetan who had courteously waited for the others to try first. He smeared some honey at one end of the tiny hole. Then he picked a wee ant, stuck the silk thread to the foot of the ant, and placed it at the opening of the other side of the flaw. Attracted by the fragrance of the honey and guided by the envoy, the ant crept into the flaw and followed the tunnel-like opening until it reached the honey on the opposite side. The envoy formed the thread into a loop suspending the jade and presented it to the king with a bow.

The emperor was very surprised and decided that he must test the clever envoy once more, so he said, "In order to treat this matter seriously and have the unsuccessful envoys accept defeat without complaint, please agree to another contest."

A carpenter was thereby ordered to shape a round stick from a big tree and taper it at each end so both ends looked equally smooth and symmetrical. Then the emperor said, "Please come forward to inspect this stick carefully. Whoever can discern which end is near the root of the tree and which is near the top, and moreover can explain why, will be the successful envoy."

The six envoys inspected the stick again and again, and measured it over and over, yet none could figure out the answer. The Tibetan envoy was from the mountainous regions and knew the forest well. Knowing that the part of the tree closer to the root was heavier than the top part, he asked to have the round stick placed in the moat around the palace. The flow of water was gentle thus allowing the round stick to float with one end dipping slightly lower than the other. The envoy then explained the reason as he understood it.

Although the emperor was pleased with the cleverness of this envoy, deep in his heart he was still reluctant to have his daughter leave for such a remote country. One of his astute ministers who understood exactly how the emperor felt, finally suggested, "Your Highness could select three hundred beautiful court ladies all dressed alike, and have the princess among them. Whichever envoy can recognize the princess will be considered the winner. This method will prove that heaven has ordained the marriage, and the princess and chieftain are destined for each other. Since no envoy has ever seen the princess, they will all probably fail. In that case the princess can remain here."

The emperor consequently announced yet one more contest: "Among three hundred maidens is the real princess. Whoever can point to her will be considered the envoy whose master is destined to marry the princess."

There was nothing to do but agree to the emperor's terms although the envoy knew in his heart that he had fulfilled the requisites of the emperor's demands three times before. The hand of the princess rightfully belonged to his own Tibetan Chieftain.

All six envoys picked out the most beautiful maiden in the group. But all were wrong. Then the Tibetan's turn came. Like the others, he had never seen the princess or had any information about her. But unlike them, he was not one to give up so easily. He vowed to succeed in his mission and tried day and night to detect anything that would serve as a clue. He pricked up his ears for the slightest gossip around the palace. Thus he questioned the most menial workers, one being the old laundress with sunken cheeks from loss of teeth.

"Oh, guest officer, what a strange job you have!" she exclaimed in a hoarse stiffled voice. "Who would dare talk! The emperor has an honorable diviner who can pinpoint anything within his powers of divination. If he knew that I gave you information, I wouldn't be here alive."

Because the envoy had much knowledge, he knew the diviner would answer in vague terms if questioned concerning the informer. He would speak of surrounding elements and of visions.

"Oh, my old aunt, please be at peace and tell me whatever you happen to know. If you follow my instructions even the most capable imperial diviner won't be able to detect a thing," he said to assure the timid old woman.

Thereupon, he took three big, white stones, placed an enormous pan on top, filled the pan with water and put a wooden bench in the water. Asking her to sit on the bench, he gave her a small copper trumpet with a silver mouthpiece and said, "Old aunt, please use this copper trumpet to speak through. If any diviner ever really succeeded in discovering anything, the most he could do would be to point out that a person who spoke had a copper mouth with silver teeth; that the speaker lived in a wooden hill and the hill was in an iron sea on top of three stone mountains. No one could possible guess where the stone mountains are nor what heavenly saint has a copper mouth with silver teeth. My old aunt, they might even call you a heavenly saint! Please don't worry."

When she heard his plan she became confident and spoke freely since she knew he already had successfully performed the required tasks and therefore deserved to win the hand of the princess for his chieftain.

"Guest officer, be sure you don't select the most beautiful maiden in the group. Although not ugly, she isn't

the most beautiful. Her beauty has been magnified ten-fold by everyone only because she is a princess. More-over, don't seek her at the beginning or end. The emperor purposely hid her near the middle. Another thing—ever since a little girl, the princess liked to put on her hair a certain fragrant lotion having honey in it. This was a gift to our emperor from a foreign lord. Only the princess was given permission to use it. Honeybees constantly buzz around her head because of the fra-grance. But she likes bees and never drives them away. So if you see any bee around a maiden's head, she is the real princess. These facts had been told by the court attendants; in turn the imperial cook heard them. The tales came to my ears through him as I do his laundry. Now guest officer, that is all I can tell you. Go and try your luck."

The Tibetan envoy thanked her and gave her a reward. Then he returned to the palace. He took care to note who was in the middle of the group and ignored the beginning and end. He deliberately walked slowly back and forth waiting for high noon when the bees usually came forth to gather honey. Truly, he noticed a little golden-colored bee buzzing around a maiden's head, and she did not seem afraid, but even glanced at it with soft, loving eyes.

"That is the real princess," the Tibetan envoy said as he stepped forth to point at her.

The ability to recognize the princess gained the respect and admiration of the other envoys, but the emperor and officials were very suspicious. No other foreign envoy had ever seen the princess. How then could he recognize her? Somebody must have told him something. Convinced that he had received help the emperor ordered the imperial diviner to find out. But the diviner only mumbled something mysterious and nothing ever came of it. Thus, the emperor had no alternative and was forced to give his daughter in marriage to the Tibetan chieftain. The Tibetan envoy was then granted an audience with the princess.

"Your Highness, Princess," the envoy said respectfully with joy in his heart. "I am truly grateful to receive the royal consent for this marriage so our chieftain may have such a gracious, virtuous queen as Your Highness. When you are ready to leave, His Majesty will undoubtedly give you a rich dowry. Please refuse all precious materials for our chieftain does not lack these things. Only ask for seeds, hoes, plows, craftsmen and carpenters. This will enable us to plow our fields and have a better living, much as your own Han people, and worth more than any dowry of gold or silver."

Wen Ch'eng did as he requested and on her departure took only the practical items valued by the Tibetans. Although the emperor thought this a strange dowry, he had five hundred pack animals loaded with seeds for planting all kinds of grains, and another thousand loaded with plows and hoes. Several hundred most skilled craftsmen and carpenters were selected to accompany the entourage. Thus the princess began her journey to Tibet. From that day forth, Tibet had better harvests and produced crafts as never before. The Han craftsmen and carpenters taught the people how to build a mill powered by a water-wheel, and even helped them in many other useful and worthwhile endeavors.

The princess was indeed a virtuous and gracious queen who loved the Tibetan chieftain dearly and brought him much happiness.

# BRIEF CHRONOLOGY OF CHINESE HISTORY

The Chinese People and The Minorities—Their Conflicts

27th Century B.C.

The first major encounter occurred when the southern tribes—the Miao, Li, Yao, T'ung, Chuang, Yi, T'ang, Lao and Thai, formed an alliance against Huang Ti. This battle was for control of the fertile Yellow River basin. The southern tribes under leadership of Ch'ih Yu, were defeated and therafter referred to as the *Nan Man,* Southern Barbarians.

Huang Ti was said to be a descendant of the Hua Hsia tribe from the northwest Yellow River Valley. According to historical records, he was China's first ruler and was called the Yellow Emperor. He was traditionally honored as the victor over the powerful outside tribes, and thus became the sovereign of the yellow earth regions along the Yellow River in (present) Shensi, Shansi, Honan, Hopei, and Shantung Provinces. He gradually extended his power southward to the Yangtze plains and the Pearl River in the extreme south. The southern tribes retreated to the hinterland, and in subsequent years, were driven even further into the undeveloped mountainous regions.

23rd Century B.C.

The Huen Yü were the earliest invaders. They occupied regions in the present Mongolian steppe, and were thought to be related to the Turks and Tatars. The were nortorious for their ferocity, and continually pillaged and devastated the land during the time of Shun. He, according to orthodox history, was one of the early rulers who created a Golden Age by his sagacious rule. This continued as Yü helped the aging Shun govern, and after the latter's death, became the ruler. Yü became known to posterity as Great Yü in recognition of his ability to cope with the floods rampant during their time, and his dedication to the task. He allegedly built walls to protect the kingdom against the Hsiung Nu incursions.

18th Century B.C.

Known as the Squatting Barbarians in antiquity, because of their squatting posture, these tribes survived in historical times as the *Tung Yi,* Eastern Barbarians. Having joined forces with the southern tribes in momentous battle that was to determine whether these tribes or the Chinese would control the territory that was then China. The Shang Dynasty kings subjugated the tribes after repeated fierce battles and revolts. After being defeated, remnants of the Squatting Barbarians migrated to what is now Shantung Province. They were later conquered and enslaved by the Shang kings whose records denoted the tribes as the Tung Yi.

3rd Century B.C.

The Hsiung Nu were just as barbarous as the Huen Yü, their forebears, and were the major opponents in the North. In European history, they were known as the Huns. Their cruelty was greatly feared by the Shang, who used the slain captives as sacrifice to their ancestors, and depicted their likeness on bronze ritual vessels. Shih Huang, an emperor of the Ch'in Dynasty, drove them into the hinterland and rebuilt and joined the walls to make The Great Wall.

2nd Century A.D.

The Western Han policy of peaceful co-existence with the Hsiung Nu by giving a princess in marriage to the Mongol Khan and sending gifts, had helped to maintain seventy years of peace. After a time, the Mongol Chieftains made increasingly oppressive and humiliating demands. When Wu Ti became the ruler, he decided to reverse the policy. More than twenty-one years of constant, violent warfare drained the Han economy, but a total victory was claimed.

When the Eastern Han was founded, the king again fought the Hsiung Nu, who had taken advantage of twenty-five years of chaos that followed Wu Ti's death. Whenever life became difficult, the Hsiung Nu would swoop down from the Mongolian steppe to the rich Yellow River plains in search of food. Even after twenty-one years fighting there was no decisive victory. Then Han Ming Ti took up the cudgels as did his son and grandson for thirty-one years; only then were the Hsiung Nu driven back to Asia Minor.

3rd to 6th Century A.D.

Known as the Period of Disunion since there were a great many dynasties and kingdoms. The *Wu Hu,* five tribes of Turks, Tatars and Mongols, invaded after the Three Kingdoms period and before the Sui Dynasty. The Sui re-united China, building the first Grand Canal and linking the existing waterways from the Yangtze to the Yellow River and then on up the Wei to Ch'ang-an, the capital.

10th Century A.D.

By the end of the T'ang Dynasty, and before the Sung Dynasty, the Khitan tribes ruled in the North. There was a succession of brief dynasties, while the south was divided between ten kingdoms. During the Sung Dynasty, the Khitan and Tartar invasions occurred and they ruled the Northern Sung. The Chinese fled to the South.

13th Century A.D.

The Mongol became very strong at the turn of the thirteenth century. Their forebears were the Hsiung Nu tribes. Under the leadership of Jenghis Khan (1206–1277 A.D.), they defeated the Tartars from Outer Mongolia, while their ally, the Chin tribes, attacked from the South. Chin was then already the master of North China, having conquered the last Sung Dynasty emperor. By 1153 A.D. the Chin had moved their capital to Yenching (present) Peking.

After Jenghis Khan died, his son broke the alliance and invaded the Chin tribes. With that, he extended his territory into North China. By the time that the Khan's grandson, Kubilai Khan became the ruler, the Mongol armies had not only marched westward as far as the Mediterranean, but conquered all of China and established the Yüan Dynasty. Being warriors by nature, they were ruthless and did not benefit by their sovereignty over China except by using it as a hinterland warehouse to support their marching armies which even reached Europe. The heavy hand of Mongol rule came to an end after only eighty-eight years. Meanwhile there was much suffering among the Chinese; because of their unhappiness, scholars turned to the theater, using drama, librettos and story telling as an outlet for their feelings. Moreover, there were a large number of scholars unemployed because the Han system of examinations had been discontinued, and they joined the ranks of impoverished discontents who turned their talents and energy to writing. Some brilliant work was created, among them, tales to arouse peoples' patriotism, to unite and drive out the hated foreign rulers.

17th Century A.D.

The Manchu were a Tungusic people from the Amur basin region. In the middle of the seventeenth century, a rebellious Ming Dynasty general betrayed the kingdom by leading the Manchu army into North China. They ultimately conquered the Ming, and established the Ch'ing Dynasty. Nevertheless, Chinese traditions and culture were retained virtually intact. In fact, many Ch'ing emperors became quite learned in varied aspects of ancient Chinese culture. The Chinese 'dragon' was even adopted as their imperial emblem. They were considerably wiser than the Mongols.

Although this dynasty never possessed the dynamic quality of creative genius of the Han, T'ang, or Sung, the government flourished under the enlightened rule of K'ang Hsi and Ch'ien Lung, both sympathetic toward the conquered Chinese. Poems composed by Ch'ien Lung to commemorate his numerous visits to places throughout his kingdom, were chiseled on stone tablets from his calligraphy. He was also a painter and patron of the arts and literature. Yet for all the vast quantity of writing and books produced during his dynasty, much was mediocre. A novel, 'The Red Chamber Dream,' (Hung Lou Meng) famed for its excellent portrayal of a large, wealthy, thoroughly degenerate family, delineated the decadence of the latter part of the dynasty. A lesser known tale *The Official and The Hermit,* contained herein, depicted another segment of society having men who actively served the emperor, but withdrew for one reason or another, and those who renounced a worldly life from the outset in favor of seclusion. Predominantly Taoist, this tale could have occurred in any one of China's many dynasties, from the periods after the Han to the Manchu.

19th Century A.D.

Near the end of the Ch'ing Dynasty, there was a strong literary movement to break away from the traditional classic manner of writing. Contemporary scholars devoted their time to compiling short stories and used conversational language to edit them. There was a trend to revive the freshness and simplicity of early folk stories; a number of tales, once oral in tradition and later enhanced by writers, were again told orally by story-tellers.

During this final dynasty the empire achieved its greatest expansion, recovering Inner Mongolia and Chinese Turkestan and for the first time including Tibet, Outer Mongolia and Taiwan.

20th Century A.D.

In 1912 with the abdication of the boy-emperor, rule by sovereigns came to an end. A republic was founded and within thirty-eight years, a socialistic nation emerged.

# GLOSSARY

Ah'ya—an exclamation of pleasure.

Ai'ya—an exclamation of fear.

Cattie—a measure of weight; one cattie equals approximately 1⅓ pounds.

Chen—old.

Chen Nan—conquer the South.

Ch'ing Tu—pure land.

Ching-ching—a courtesy phrase meaning "You lead the way, I will follow."

Chung-nan—extreme South.

Ee-e—an exclamation of surprise, wonder.

E-ya—an exclamation of unpleasantness, distaste.

Fai—not; added to a name it means one is not what one's name implies.

Ho! Haw!—an exclamation used when driving animals.

Joss stick—a slender stick of incense burned before a Chinese God.

Kowtow—to kneel and touch the forehead to the ground as a token of homage, worship or respect.

Kung Kung—Grand Uncle.

Kwon—pot or container.

Li—a unit of distance, one li equals approximately ⅓ mile.

Nan Man—southern barbarians.

O Mi To Fu—a Buddhist incantation.

P'i p'a—a four stringed musical instrument used to accompany a folktale.

Shan—mountain.

Si-sa—a noise used to describe something disintegrating.

Tael—a unit of value based upon the value of a tael weight of silver.

Tai—big; added to a name it means eldest.

Tao Te Ching—*The Way and Virtuous Path of Tao.*

Tsamba—a flour made from parched ground barley, the chief cereal food of Tibet.

T'u-teng—a totem - an emblem of family or clan, often regarded as a reminder of ancestory having religious significance.

Wan Shui—ten thousand years, also used to indicate unlimited or countless.

Wang Fu Shan—Awaiting Husband Hill in Kowloon along the Kwangtung border.

Wei—a word used as a means of getting a person's attention, similar to "hello."

Yamen—an official building, used as a magistrate's office, often his residence.

Yen—salt.

Yu I—meaning Friendship or Goodwill Pass. A pass through the mountains in the south of Kwangsi Province.

Yurt—a circular domed tent of skins stretched over a collapsible lattice framework used by Mongol Nomads.

# MAP OF CHINA

SINKIANG ULGHUR

KANSU

JAMMU AND KASMIR

TSINGHAI

Yangtze River

Saiween River

TIBET

NEPAL

BHUTAN

INDIA

BURMA

THAILAND

UNION OF SOVIET
SOCIALIST REPUBLICS

MONGOLIA

HEILUNGKIANG

Ch'ang-ch'un

KIRIN

INNER MONGOLIA

LIAONING

NORTH KOREA

SOUTH KOREA

Peking

NINGHSIA HUI A.R.

HOPEH

SHANSI

Yellow River

SHANTUNG

KIANGSU

SHENSI

HONAN

ANHWEI

Nanking

Shanghai

HUPEH

CHWAN

Yangtze River

CHEKIANG

EAST
CHINA
SEA

Nan-ch'ang

HUNAN

KIANGSI

Foochow

KWEICHOW

FUKIEN

FORMOSA STRAIT

Taipei

TAIWAN

-ming

KWANGSI
CHUANG
A.R.

KWANGTUNG

NNAN

Pearl River

Canton

Nan-ning

NORTH
VIETNAM

HONG KONG
(U.K.)

MACAO
(Port.)

OS

HAINAN

SOUTH
CHINA
SEA

175

## BOOKS BY CELESTIAL ARTS
*of special interest to students and teachers*


**GAMES STUDENTS PLAY**, Ken Ernst
*and what to do about them*
17-0    paper    $3.95

**THE COMPLETE BOOK OF GINSENG**, Richard Heffern
*botany, history, applications and legends*
151-5    paper    $3.95

**HAIKU REVISITED**, Louis Cuneo
*traditional Japanese poetry including discussion of form*
14-4    paper    $3.95

**HONG KONG: Customs and Culture**, Duane Rubin
*A Travel Enjoyment Book*
071-3    paper    $4.95

**JAPAN:  Customs and Culture**, Duane Rubin
*A Travel Enjoyment Book*
04-7    paper    $4.95

**WELLS FARGO  THE LEGEND**, Dale Robertson
*legends based in fact on the American West*
064-0    paper    $4.95

**WILDFLOWERS OF THE WEST**, Mabel Crittenden and
                                Dorothy Telfer
*new and unique method of identifying and studying
wildflowers*
069-1    paper    $4.95